AIR FRYER Cookbook

with pictures

1000+ Days of Simple, Quick & Delicious Recipes to Fry, Bake and Grill Your Favourite Meals. 21 Tips & Tricks to Effortlessly Become a Pro

FULL COLOR EDITION

Shaelyn Alexa

Shaelyn Alexa © Copyright 2022 - All rights reserved.
The content contained within this book may not be reproduced, duplicated or transmitted without direct written permission from the author or the publisher. Under no circumstances will any blame or legal responsibility be held against the publisher, or author, for any damages, reparation, or monetary loss due to the information contained within this book. Either directly or indirectly.

Legal Notice:
This book is copyright protected. This book is only for personal use. You cannot amend, distribute, sell, use, quote or paraphrase any part, or the content within this book, without the consent of the author or publisher.

Disclaimer Notice:
Please note the information contained within this document is for educational and entertainment purposes only. All effort has been executed to present accurate, up to date, and reliable, complete information. No warranties of any kind are declared or implied. Readers acknowledge that the author is not engaging in the rendering of legal, financial, medical or professional advice. The content within this book has been derived from various sources. Please consult a licensed professional before attempting any techniques outlined in this book.
By reading this document, the reader agrees that under no circumstances is the author responsible for any losses, direct or indirect, which are incurred as a result of the use of information contained within this document, including, but not limited to, — errors, omissions, or inaccuracies.

Table of Contents

Introduction | 5

The basics of the air fryer | 6

How the air fryer works | 9

Air fryer maintenance | 14

Practical tips for using the air fryer | 16

Breakfast | 19

Snacks and Appetizers | 23

Beef, Pork and Lamb | 28

Poultry | 38

Seafood | 49

Vegetables and Salad | 60

Measurements Conversion | 71

Recipes Index | 72

Conclusion | 74

Introduction

If we think about good food every day, and especially about which food or which recipes are the absolute tastiest, we certainly cannot fail to refer to stir-fries.

What could taste better than a plate of French fries?

The problem arises, as is well known, when it is thought that frying, especially if abused, is definitely not a good ally of health, and in a particular way it is not among the main choices useful in the pursuit of healthy eating and shedding excess pounds.

After this premise, now the question arises, whether there is a solution that combines the pleasure of fried food with maintaining a healthy diet, without excess fat...

The answer to this dilemma seems to have been created on purpose.

One of the greatest advances concerning, in fact, the food, culinary and technological spheres has been proposed by a rather recent invention.

We are really talking about the air fryer.

This new invention basically allows frying without oil, but to achieve the same result as oil frying, by means of a very hot jet of air.

What this means, then, is that the foods you are going to prepare with the air fryer will turn out, just like those fried normally, basically crispy on the outside and soft on the inside.

Put another way, the air fryer simulates cooking with oil without submerging food in it, also in some ways representing a halfway solution between oil frying and baking. But air fryers usually allow us to achieve light frying that is not bad for our figure or our body.

Thanks to them and, as we will see in the course of this discussion, different types of cooking can be achieved, such as grilling or baking.

As the market is supplied with different types of air fryers, different types of electric heating elements, it is therefore possible to vary cooking and types of dishes that will be brought to the table.

After this brief introduction you will find, in the first chapter, an even more detailed description of the main features and advantages of this particular household appliance.

The second chapter will explain its operation and mistakes to avoid while using it in the kitchen.

The third chapter will explain the maintenance and cleaning of the air fryer while, in the fourth chapter, tricks and practical tips will be given to make the best use of it.

After this more theoretical part, a more practical part will be covered extensively.

This practical part illustrated in the final chapters, will be represented by all the recipes that can be created through the use of the fryer, ranging from breakfast to dinner, from fish to desserts

The basics of the air fryer

What is the air fryer?

Before delving directly into the working mechanism of the air fryer, it is deemed necessary to understand in more detail what exactly this particular type of "cooking machine" is.

If a brief description of the air fryer was given in the introduction, we will now go on to understand its *sketch* in detail.

As mentioned then in the introduction itself, it is well known that The Fried is as good as it is unhealthy.

We asked ourselves, then, is it necessary to give it up? Not necessarily, and the dilemma can be solved through this very innovation.

Thus, it is well established that with the air fryer it is possible to fry without oil, and therefore lighter.

We are aware that the major innovation brought by the air fryer is precisely to replace unhealthy frying with a much lighter and healthier variant.

But what are we talking about when we mention this particular ally in the kitchen?

What then is the air fryer?

When we talk about an air fryer, we commonly refer to a small countertop convection oven that is designed and has as its main purpose, to simulate oil cooking, as mentioned above, without submerging the food in the oil itself.

This small oven, through a fan that circulates hot air at high speed, produces a crispy layer in the food through a browning process.

The hot air fryer or commonly known as an oil-free fryer, is, therefore, a machine that allows food to be fried not with fat (oil or butter) but with heat accumulated in the cooking chamber.

In a few simple words, the air fryer represents one of the most innovative kitchen tools that have been put on the market today.

It is also a unique innovation because it will not only allow you to be able to bring healthier food to your table, but its uniqueness comes from the cooking mechanism itself.

This means that while other appliances that are commonly used in the kitchen tend to use the "conduction process" for cooking, the air fryer will instead exploit the "convection" technique which uses the circulation of hot, rapid air to cause, as we said above, the food to brown and thus cook.

Basically, an air fryer is like a small electric ventilated oven, with the advantage that it can remove much more moisture from the food and ensure a crispier, drier result.

It thus offers the same performance as any ordinary deep fryer but, thanks to its innovative technology, allows us to enjoy the dishes we so enjoy without taking in all the fat (normally harmful to our health).

Of course, to some people it might seem very strange to have fried food "without oil."

One possible option would be to add a teaspoon of oil, just to give a little flavor, without compromising, however, the wholesomeness of the dish cooked by means of this tool.

On the exact operation of this machinery will be discussed in detail in the next chapter.

The main features of the air fryer

Having made a brief introduction of the air fryer, it is appropriate, now, to describe its main features to understand it in more detail.

What are the main features of this innovative kitchen tool?

We know that its main feature is cooking without oil and fat. But if we talk about specific and technical characteristics, we must first say that there are a variety of types, sizes, strengths and capacities on the market.

In terms of form, the air fryer can be presented either horizontally or vertically but almost always comes with additional accessories and features.

If, on the other hand, we talk about the main features that more or less unite all air fryers on the market, it is necessary to list them as follows:

- **Digital screen (touch system):** every air fryer has, and it is perhaps one of the main peculiarities of it, a screen with a totally touch screen function. This type of system makes it possible to adjust functionality (temperature, cooking mode and time) in the easiest way possible.
- **Automatic temperature control system:** thanks to this system, it is possible for the air fryer to track the temperature and lock it if the set temperature is reached.
- **Beeper:** thanks to a beeper that beeps when the preset timer expires, you can do more in the kitchen and know exactly when our dish is ready.
- **Different cooking settings:** this is probably, although it shares it quite a lot with the fan oven, one of the most important innovations brought by this tool. The wide range of predefined cooking and settings (ranging from grilling to baking) allows us to be able to achieve the desired cooking for each and every dish we choose to prepare.

Regarding, however, the component-level

features of an air fryer, assuming that there are different types, capacities, and capacities, they almost all share these accessories:

- Frying pan
- Basket
- Basket handle
- Basket release button
- Ignition light
- Heating light
- Timer
- Ignition knob
- Temperature control knob
- Air inlet
- Air outlet openings
- Power cable

The advantages of the air fryer

Having described, in the preceding paragraphs, the main features concerning the air fryer and, reiterating several times its extraordinary innovation in the culinary field, it seems appropriate at this point to list all its possible advantages.

- Health-level benefits: impossible not to mention first the benefits brought to our diet and, consequently, to our health. There is nothing better, than fried "without being fried," which, as mentioned earlier, not only benefits our health, but also our fitness itself. As far as health is concerned, specifically, in addition to our liver (which struggles to get rid of the excess fat from fried foods), the minimal fat intake will be crucial for our heart and blood circulation. Having this as one of main advantages, the air fryer also becomes a key ally for those who practice sports and need to follow a low-calorie dietary regimen.
- **Safe frying:** the air fryer is designed for safe frying. This means that by not being forced to operate with boiling oil, the risk of burns is also avoided. In addition, thanks to one of the main features listed in the previous paragraph, the preset timer, it will automatically turn off as soon as the cooking time is reached.
- **Versatility and ease of use:** with different cooking settings, you can choose which one is most congenial to the recipes you want to prepare. These preset cooking programs are also designed for beginners to make it easier for them to prepare dishes in the kitchen. Coupled with all these advantages, there is also the ease of cleaning, thanks to the fact that no oils are used, so there is hardly any extra residue left inside the fryer itself.
- **Eco-friendly cooking and environmental friendliness:** by reducing cooking time and oil used, this tool saves energy and, most importantly, avoids oil disposal. All this benefits our planet.
- Not to mention, taking up little space, it allows you to reorganize your kitchen in the best possible way.
- **Reduce odors:** we know that one of the main complaints when frying with oil is to infest the house with a bad smell. The air fryer can remedy this problem as well.

After making a list of the features and benefits brought by the air fryer we will go into the discussion regarding the working mechanism of this valuable ally in the kitchen in the next chapter.

How the air fryer works

Air fryer operation and settings

Now that we have a fairly clear idea of what the air fryer is and what its main features are, we can introduce the discussion of its operation and settings (buttons and functions).

The most logical thing to think of is, that if we are talking about an "air" fryer, its operation cannot but be separated from the concept (precisely because the name itself says so) of cooking by air jet.

As mentioned at the beginning of the previous chapter, the major innovation brought by this cooking tool is precisely the method, the technique that is used to cook, compared to the cooking methods already known and used on a daily basis.

All of these traditional cooking tools and devices take advantage of the conduction technique and thus (like, for example, the oven) employ a radiator that transfers the heat necessary for the food to cook.

The main difference and novelty introduced with the air fryer is precisely the method used to cook: in fact, it uses the convection technique.

This means that it takes advantage of the circulation of hot air in the food we are cooking.

In other words, the air fryer elevates the temperature of the air being circulated through the food.

Air is basically sucked into the inlet chamber allowing this instrument to reach a high temperature in a short time.

The air fryer, therefore, completely disrupts the notion that oil constitutes the sine qua non for achieving fast and perfect frying.

And it does so by equal process: if oil heats up in a short time and allows easy cooking at high temperatures, the air fryer does so just as quickly and easily by means of air as the heat carrier.

In order for this to happen, and referring to the discussion of one of the main components of this kitchen tool and that is the cooking chamber inside it-thanks to this very chamber, the air is heated and circulated very quickly, so as to ensure even frying of food.

It has been calculated that the air circulating inside this chamber can reach as high as 200 degrees Celsius temperature (optimal temperature for frying, but without all the contraindications of normal frying with oil or other fats).

Of course, it is more than fair to remind you that when you have decided to purchase and employ an air fryer, it is necessary to follow all the instructions given in the enclosed booklet and to take all the precautions indicated.

That said, as for the buttons and functions related to the air fryer, let us reiterate that it was a tool designed primarily for beginners in the kitchen, so we are talking about functions and buttons designed to be used in the simplest way possible.

In order to start cooking our food, it is first necessary to place all the necessary ingredients in the basket (some have pans or even baking pans).

After that all our buttons will come to the rescue so that we can cook and finish our dishes.

The moment we place the ingredients in the basket, it is necessary to press the main power button (which is usually shaped like the classic play).

When power on occurs, the timer button that adjusts the timing we want to set along with the button that adjusts the temperature will light up.

Cooking time and temperature will be given in the various recipes each time.

In addition to these classic buttons, there are also so-called "function buttons"-these buttons will allow you to change cooking methods to your liking.

You will be able to find sweet, grilling (especially for meat and fish), baking, and regular frying function.

To recap, the main settings of the air fryer are as follows:

> **Temperature selection:** i.e., the ability to set, by light button, the cooking temperature (with a range usually from 160 to 200 degrees)
> **Timer:** via the special light button (a very important function) there is an obligation to set a timing and adjust it according to the desired cooking (which is not the case with other kitchen appliances with automatic and preset programs).
> **Beeps and automatic shutdown:** when temperature and cooking time are reached, the air fryer will warn you and shut down automatically
> **Different cooking functions:** as we have already mentioned, this kitchen tool offers a variety of cooking such as, grill, dessert cooking, oven function and frying.

Having closed the discussion of operation and functions, we feel it is also fair to mention the discussion regarding the power and energy consumption of the air fryer.

In terms of power, they can start from a

minimum of 1400 to a maximum of 2000 watts.

But the main problem, and here we are connected to the discussion of power consumption, is not the power itself.

Air fryers are generally relatively low-power appliances, but some have power that allows them to reach high temperatures in a matter of minutes (even some get there in two, three minutes maximum).

But despite this, its consumption remains lower than that of conventional ovens, representing, as mentioned earlier, a big advantage in terms of energy savings.

How to solve the main problems in using the air fryer?

It is possible that some problems may arise while using the air fryer.

This section will then report the most common problems related to the use of this kitchen tool, combined with a possible solution.

You will be shown, in practice, a short comprehensive guide to solving these various issues. We have schematized them for you as below:

PROBLEM	POSSIBLE SOLUTION
The outside of the device becomes too hot after use	This is a rather normal phenomenon, due precisely to the circulation of warm air, but rest assured that the knobs will still remain cold
The device does not turn on or does not work properly	Make sure the power outlet is well connected and that the timer and temperature are set correctly
Food cooking is not optimal	Try distributing less quantity of ingredients (or more evenly perhaps by stirring more often or shaking the basket occasionally) and try cooking smaller portions (always check temperature and cooking time).
The basket is not introduced well and the fryer does not start	Make sure that you have not exceeded the limits of ingredients that can be inserted into the basket and try to insert it properly into the slot until you hear a click of interlocking
White smoke is coming out of my fryer	There is probably some oil residue left over from previous fry-ups or you have used too much oil. Be sure to remove any oily or fatty residue. These residues, in addition to oil could be previous panings or the fat from the meat. It is always very important to keep the fryer clean for future cooking

Mistakes to avoid

After focusing on the operation and troubleshooting of problems that can arise when cooking with an air fryer, it is important to keep in mind that there are mistakes to avoid.

To be avoided as, being an electrical appliance anyway that can be exposed to breakage or damage. Or to prevent your food from not being cooked properly or evenly. Among the most important mistakes to avoid regarding damage or breakage are the following:

› Remember to put the ingredients to be fried in the basket so that they do not come in contact with the heating elements.
› Do not cover the air circulation openings while the unit is in operation.
› Do not fill the container with so much oil to avoid the danger of fire.
› Do not immerse the device in water or other liquids or rinse it under running water.
› Before connecting the appliance, check that the voltage shown on the plug matches the available voltage.
› Do not use the appliance if the plug, power cord or the appliance itself is damaged.
› In case the power cord is damaged, it should be replaced, to avoid dangerous situations.
› This equipment may be used by children 8 years of age and older and by persons with reduced mental, physical or sensory capabilities who lack appropriate experience or knowledge, provided they have received assistance or training in using the equipment safely and are aware of the potential hazards associated with such use.
› Prevent children from playing with the device.
› Keep the power cord away from glowing surfaces.
› Connect the device to a grounding outlet only.
› Always make sure the plug is properly inserted into the power outlet.
› Always place and use the device on a flat, stable and horizontal surface.
› This unit is not designed to be used in conjunction with an external timer or a separate system with remote control.
› Do not place the device against a wall or another appliance.
› Leave at least 10 cm clearance at the back and sides and 10 cm clearance above the appliance. Do not place any objects on top of the appliance.
› During hot air frying, steam is emitted through the air circulation openings. Therefore, it is very important to keep hands and face at a safe distance from steam and air circulation openings. Pay attention to steam and hot air also when removing the container from the appliance.
› Accessible surfaces may become very hot during use. Be careful when handling them.
› In order to ensure optimal operation, make sure before each use of the device that the heating element and its surroundings are clean and free of food or oil residues.
› Do not place the appliance above or near gas stoves or any type of electric stove or hotplate, or inside heated ovens.
› Do not include ingredients with low weight.
› Never touch the inside of the device while it is in operation.
› Do not place the appliance on or near combustible material, such as tablecloths and curtains.

- Unplug the appliance immediately if dark smoke is coming out of it. Wait for no more smoke to come out of the appliance before removing the container
- After this short list that is more about the mistakes to avoid for your safety and security, we now list the mistakes to avoid when using the air fryer for cooking.
- Make sure you have enough space to allow your air fryer to "breathe"
- As for pans and baskets, choose light-colored ones, because black may absorb even more heat, creating unevenness in cooking
- As mentioned earlier, avoid overusing oil and take care to clean the fryer after each use.
- Don't forget not to overdo the ingredients and, shake the basket from time to time for optimal cooking.

Air fryer maintenance

How to do air fryer maintenance and cleaning

Having explained, in the previous chapters, the operation and mistakes to avoid when using the air fryer, it is considered essential, at this point in the discussion, to illustrate the cleaning and maintenance of this kitchen tool.

The durability and performance of this instrument logically depend on maintaining its optimal state.

This means that your air fryer should be as clean and free of encrusted debris as possible.

In general, air fryers are fairly easy to keep clean, all the more so when compared to classic oil fryers.

It should also be mentioned that, as far as the container basket is concerned, most models have the option of washing the baskets directly in the dishwasher.

A very important thing to remember, especially to maintain, as mentioned above, its operation-as well as for proper cleaning-is to let the fryer cool completely before cleaning it completely.

If there should be any stubborn grease residue, such as from the fattest meats, it would be much better to let the baskets soak for a while, filling them with hot water and degreasing soap until the grease has partially dissolved

After this small "prewash" you can proceed either by hand washing or directly in the dishwasher.

It is also most important to keep in mind that the heating element must also be cleaned, as it can be perfectly reached by food splashes, every time we use the air fryer.

As for the cleaning tool, it is strongly recommended to use a damp, soft cloth to clean both the heating element and the exterior.

Therefore, it is always best to use microfiber cloths or sponges.

On the other hand, regarding the removal of any fouling, it must be remembered that the watchword is always the same, and that is: delicacy.

So, never scrub your air fryer with abrasive sponges or use harsh products that could damage it.

How to remove, on the other hand, any food odors?

It may happen, perhaps by cooking fish, for example, that some smell remains inside your air fryer.

A possible solution to remedy this problem would be to put half a glass of wine vinegar in the bottom of the outer basket, along with about half a liter of water and raise the temperature of the fryer to the maximum.

At this point, then set the air fryer to 200° for about 10 minutes, until the liquid inside the basket has completely evaporated.

Another possible solution would be to use fresh rosemary branches.

You must always place them in the inner basket, and set the temperature to 180 degrees for 10 minutes.

It is vital here, however, to always check that the rosemary does not touch the heating element during the process.

Having pointed out these solutions and, recapping the process of cleaning your air fryer, we can summarize the process itself in a few simple steps:

› Before starting your routine cleaning, make sure the power outlet is unplugged and the fryer has completely cooled down.
› Clean the outside of the air fryer with a cloth and mild detergent
› Clean the inner basket (or tray), again with mild detergent and cloth (remember that if grease residue is present to soak it with warm water and dish soap)
› For the inside, always remember to clean them too gently with water and a soft sponge.

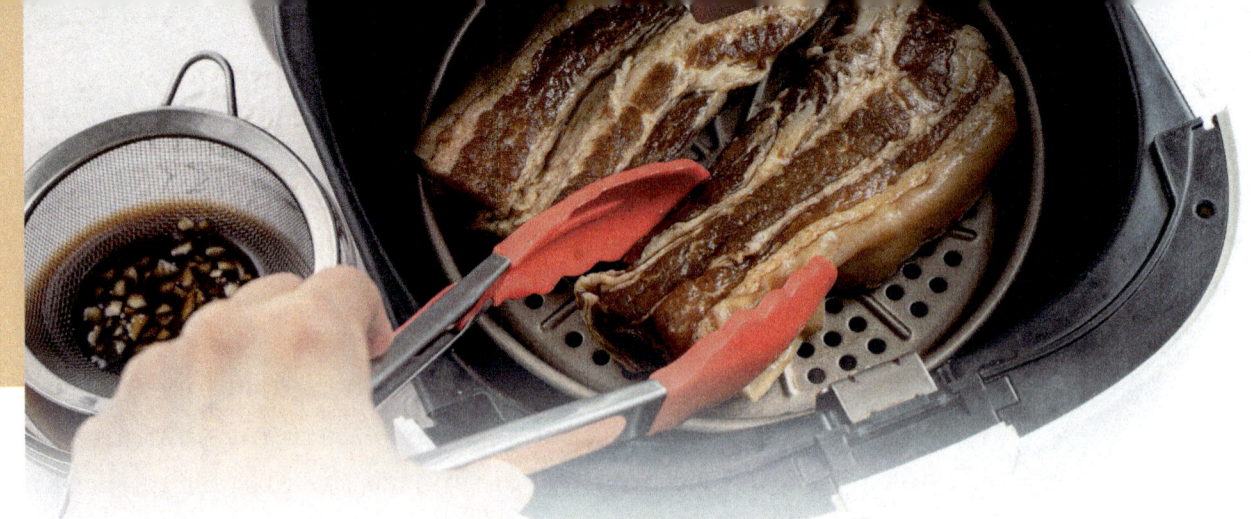

Practical tips for using the air fryer

21 tips and tricks to make the best use of your air fryer

Having come to this point in the discussion, we are well acquainted with what an air fryer is, how it works and its maintenance to enable its longevity.

If in the second chapter you were offered a list of mistakes to avoid when using this small appliance, the following will list 21 tips that will show you how to best employ it.

1. If you want to get perfect fries.

If you want to get perfectly golden and crispy fries, soak them previously (already cut) in cold water for about 20 minutes. Afterwards, dry them and sprinkle them with a little oil before placing it in the air fryer

2. To prevent steam accumulation during cooking

To remedy this inconvenience, be sure to dry your ingredients perfectly before placing it in your fryer

3. For even and optimal baking of cakes and cookies

When you decide to cook cakes with your air fryer, do not forget to cover them with a lid or aluminum foil so that the top of the cake will not burn. It would also be ideal, to cook cakes with the air fryer to purchase a steel or nonstick mold. Therefore, it is best to avoid, silicone or disposable molds.

4. Always check the cooking of food

Since each air fryer varies in its specific characteristics, it is advisable to empirically evaluate and compare the various cooking as you use it. All the more reason to always check the cooking temperature during first uses.

5. Check the cooking time

As mentioned above, each air fryer has features that unite them but also some that differ from each other, so it is a good idea to check the cooking time of each individual dish and add or subtract minutes the next times.

6. Preheat the fryer

It is a well-known fact that any ingredient we employ in our recipes (to be best cooked) must be, most of the time, preheated. Therefore, our air fryers should be preheated to achieve even cooking. If your air fryer does not have a preheat setting, simply set it to the desired temperature and let it run for about 3 minutes before placing the food directly into it.

7. Use a little oil for crispy dishes

If your food already has some natural fat (such as chicken meat, ground beef and fatty cuts of meat, etc.), then you probably do not need the oil. Whereas if it's vegetables, or dry foods, a teaspoon of oil is recommended to make sure they achieve the ideal crispness.

8. Grease the basket of your air fryer as well.

Even if your food does not require oil, always take a moment to grease (just a little) the basket of your air fryer. You can do this by rubbing, or spraying, a little oil on the bottom grates. This will ensure that your food will not stick

9. Sprinkle a little oil halfway through cooking.

Sprinkling the oil halfway through cooking will result in your food becoming crispier

10. Don't overdo the ingredients

This was already mentioned as a mistake to avoid. If you want your fried foods to turn out crispy, you must always be careful not to overload the basket. Also, to avoid uneven cooking, cook your food in different batches and, if the matter becomes constant, invest in a larger air fryer

11. Shake the basket to achieve even firings

When frying smaller items, such as chicken wings, fries etc., you will need to shake the basket occasionally to ensure even cooking.

Once we open the basket to shake, the air fryer will temporarily pause, but will resume cooking food at the same temperature one the moment we insert the basket again.

12. Use a rapid-temperature thermometer for cooking meat

This is sound advice not only for air fryer cooking but for any way you decide to cook meat.

Having a good quality quick-read thermometer is of paramount importance when it comes to cooking certain types of meats.

13. Tricks to prevent white smoke from escaping

If white smoke is coming out of your air fryer (as we indicated earlier) you have probably overdone the oil.

It will be sufficient, in this case, to stop cooking and try to wipe off excess oil.

14. Avoid putting liquids inside the basket.

If you have to cook fish in foil, for example, try to put all the liquid components of the marinade inside the foil that will contain the protein.

15. Store the preset of the recipe you like

The moment you find (even within this book) a recipe that you like and, after trying it, realize that it is cooked perfectly, you can set it in the preset of your air fryer. This means storing the timer and temperature so that it will be easier for you to cook it the next time.

16. Follow the recipes but adapt them to your context

Remember to follow the portions and recipe directions, although, as mentioned above, you can empirically check cooking times and temperatures if they do not match perfectly.

17. Air and space for your fryer

It is most important to remember that the fryer must be able to take in enough air for proper operation, so be sure to store it in a large enough space.

18. Invest in a larger capacity deep fryer if you cook for many people

Most air fryers have a capacity of 3 liters, which allows you to cook food of a capacity for about 4 people. If you have to cook for many more people, or you have occasions when you have to cook many quantities of food, the best advice is to buy an air fryer with a larger capacity and size.

19. Choose the lowest air fryer power if you don't want a big energy expenditure

Generally, you can buy fryers that take advantage of a maximum power rating of 1400 watts (or slightly higher), which will still ensure reliability, safety and guarantees on the functioning of every mechanical part of the instrument. Since the power is lower, you will not have a large energy expenditure.

20. Buy extra accessory kits if you want to indulge in recipes

You can also find useful accessory kits for cooking sweet and savory foods on the market, such as: hinged cake pans, rotisserie, pizza pan, and more.

21. About cakes and desserts

To conclude the discussion of tips, we would like to point you to one last one that concerns desserts and especially cakes. Always start from a lower temperature to bake them (as well as cover them, as mentioned before) of maximum 160 degrees. When cooked, increase by 180 degrees (the last 5 minutes) to get them perfectly crispy on the outside and soft on the inside.

Having concluded the discussion on the tips, and thus on the theoretical part of the fryer we can speak to the practical part with all the recipes you can cook with this innovative kitchen tool.

Breakfast
— RECIPES —

Best Air-Fried English Breakfast

Preparation Time: 5 minutes
Cooking Time: 20 minutes
Servings: 2

Ingredients:

- 8 sausages
- 8 bacon slices
- 4 eggs
- 1 (16-ounce) can of baked beans
- 8 slices of toast

Directions:

1. Add sausages and bacon slices to your fryer and cook 10 minutes at a 320 degrees Fahrenheit.
2. Using a ramekin or heat-safe bowl, Add baked beans, then place another ramekin and Add eggs and whisk.
3. Increase temperature to 290 degrees Fahrenheit.
4. Place it inside your air fryer and cook additional 10 minutes or until everything is done.

Nutrition: Calories 850 Fat 40g Carbs 20g Protein 48g

Breakfast Grilled Ham and Cheese

Preparation Time: 5 minutes
Cooking Time: 10 minutes
Servings: 2

Ingredients:

- 1 teaspoon butter
- 4 slices bread
- 4 slices smoked country ham
- 4 slices Cheddar cheese
- 4 thick slices tomato

Directions:

1. Spread ½ teaspoon of butter onto one side of 2 slices of bread. Each sandwich will have 1 slice of bread with butter and 1 slice without.
2. Assemble each sandwich by layering 2 slices of ham, 2 slices of cheese, and 2 slices of tomato on the unbuttered pieces of bread. Top with the other bread slices, buttered side up.
3. Place sandwiches in fryer buttered side down. Cook 4 minutes
4. Open fryer. Flip grilled cheese sandwiches. Cook additional4 minutes. Cool before serving. Cut each sandwich in half and enjoy.

Nutrition: Calories 525 Fat 25g Carbs 34g Protein 41

Breakfast Scramble Casserole

Preparation Time: 20 minutes
Cooking Time: 10 minutes
Servings: 2
Ingredients:
- 6 slices bacon
- 6 eggs
- Salt
- Pepper
- Cooking oil
- ½ cup chopped red bell pepper
- ½ cup chopped green bell pepper
- ½ cup chopped onion
- ¾ cup shredded Cheddar cheese

Directions:
1. Cook bacon, 5 to 7 minutes, flipping too evenly crisp. Dry out on paper towels, crumble, and set aside. In a medium bowl, Whisk eggs. Add salt and pepper to taste.
2. Spray barrel pan with cooking oil. Make sure to cover the bottom and sides of the pan. Add beaten eggs, crumbled bacon, red bell pepper, green bell pepper, and onion to the pan. Place pan in the air fryer. Cook 6 minutes Open fryer and Sprinkle cheese over the casserole. Cook additional 2 minutes. Cool before serving.

Nutrition: Calories 348 Fat 26g Carbs 4g Protein 25g

Cheesy Tater Tot Breakfast Bake

Preparation Time: 5 minutes
Cooking Time: 20 minutes
Servings: 2
Ingredients:
- 4 eggs
- 1 cup milk
- 1 teaspoon onion powder
- Salt
- Pepper
- Cooking oil
- 12 ounces ground chicken sausage
- 1-pound frozen tater tots
- ¾ cup shredded Cheddar cheese

Directions:
1. Whisk eggs. Add milk, onion powder, and salt and pepper to taste. Stir to combine.
2. Spray skillet with cooking oil and set over medium-high heat. Add ground sausage. Break the sausage into smaller pieces. Cook 3 to 4 minutes, until the sausage is brown. Remove from heat and set aside.
3. Spray barrel pan with cooking oil. Place tater tots in the barrel pan. Cook 6 minutes
4. Open fryer and shake the pan, then Add egg mixture and cooked sausage. Cook additional 6 minutes. Open fryer and Sprinkle cheese over tater tot bake. Cook additional 2 to 3 minutes. Cool before serving.

Nutrition: Calories 518 Fat 30g Carbs 31g Protein 30g

Classic Hash Browns

Preparation Time: 15 minutes
Cooking Time: 20 minutes
Servings: 2
Ingredients:
- 4 russet potatoes
- 1 teaspoon paprika
- Salt
- Pepper
- Cooking oil

Directions:
1. Peel potatoes. Grate potatoes. If your grater has different-size holes, use the area of the tool with the largest holes.
2. Let sit potatoes for 5 minutes in cold water.
3. Dry out potatoes and dry with paper towels or napkins. Make sure the potatoes are completely dry.
4. Season potatoes with the paprika and salt and pepper to taste. Spray potatoes with cooking oil and Transfer m to the air fryer. Cook 20 minutes and shake the basket every 5 minutes (a total of 4 times). Cool before serving.

Nutrition: Calories 150 Carbs 34g Fat 35g Protein 4g

Creamy and cheesy pancake

Preparation Time: 10 minutes
Cooking Time: 4 minutes
Servings: 2
Ingredients:
- 2 cups cream cheese
- 2 eggs
- 1 pack stevia
- 1/2 tsp. Cinnamon

Directions:
1. Preheat fryer 330 degrees f. Place eggs and stevia in a bowl.
2. Whisk until stevia is dissolved. Add cream cheese and cinnamon to eggs.
3. Whisk until smooth. Ladle the quarter of the batter into the air fryer.
4. Cook 2 minutes at 330 degrees f. Flip pancake and then Cook 2 minutes more. Repeat the process.

Nutrition: Calories 180 Fat 18g Carbs 16g Protein 15g

Snacks and Appetizers

– RECIPES –

Apple and Greek Yogurt Cake Baked

Preparation Time: 15 minutes
Cooking Time: 25 minutes
Servings: 2
Ingredients:

- 3 eggs
- 120 g caster sugar
- 150 g Greek yogurt
- 80 ml Seed oil
- 40 ml Milk
- 200 g 00 flour
- 50 g Potato starch
- 1 sachet Baking powder
- to taste cinnamon powder
- 2 teaspoons granulated sugar
- 1 red apple
- For Air Fryer XL format:
- 2 eggs
- 80 g caster sugar
- 100 g Greek yogurt
- 50 ml Oil
- 30 ml Milk
- 150 g flour
- 30 g Potato starch
- 1 sachet of baking powder

Directions:

1. Beat eggs with the sugar using the electric whisk until frothy and swollen. Then Add Greek yogurt and incorporate it with the whisk at reduced speed. Add milk and oil and always mix with the whisk. Finally, Add flour, potato starch and baking powder, incorporating them until a fluid mixture is obtained.
2. Pour mixture into a 20 cm mold, if necessary greased and floured. Cut apple into slices, if you prefer you can also peel it. Arrange m in rays on the dough. Sprinkle surface with powdered cinnamon mixed with granulated sugar.

Buckwheat and Forest Berries Cake Gluten Free and Lactose Free

Preparation Time: 10 minutes
Cooking Time: 30 minutes
Servings: 2
Ingredients:

- 2 eggs
- 100 g brown sugar
- 200 g buckwheat flour
- 50 g potato starch
- 100 g soy cream
- 120 g berries
- 10 g baking powder

Directions:

1. Beat eggs with brown sugar until a frothy mixture is obtained. Add liquid cream while continuing to whip.
2. Add buckwheat flour and potato starch little by little. Then also Add baking powder.
3. After incorporating the flours, you can Combine berries (fresh or frozen, as you prefer) with a spatula so as not to break them, leaving some of them for decoration on the surface.
4. Pour rather thick mixture into a 22 cm cake mold suitable for the air fryer basket. Place mold on the basket and operate it at 160 ° then cook it for about 35 minutes doing the toothpick test.

Nutrition: Calories: 163; Fat:2g; Protein:48g; Carbs::20g

Chocolate and Hazelnut Cake

Preparation Time: 10 minutes
Cooking Time: 25 minutes
Servings: 22
Ingredients:

- 3 eggs
- 100 g caster sugar
- 220 g flour
- 30 g bitter cocoa
- 50 ml lactose-free milk
- 40 ml Seed oil
- 1 sachet Baking powder
- 80 g whole hazelnuts

Directions:

1. Whip eggs with the sugar with the electric whisk for a few minutes until foamy. Add milk and oil flush, mixing with low speed electric whisk. Then Add flour and the bitter cocoa by sieving them.
2. When mixture is fluid, also Add baking powder. The dough is ready. Pour dough into a 22 cm diameter cake mold that enters the air fryer basket. Level it well.
3. Add whole toasted hazelnuts to the surface, just chopped. Cook in fryer at 160 ° for 15 minutes and then at 180 ° for another 10 minutes. Always check with a toothpick after at least 20 minutes. If it still seems undercooked, continue for a few minutes.
4. Bake in preheated oven at 180 ° in static mode for about 40 minutes, always making the toothpick test.

Nutrition: Calories: 453; Fat:14g; Protein:29g; Carbs::14g

Donut Cream and Almonds

Preparation Time: 10 minutes
Cooking Time: 20 minutes
Servings: 2
Ingredients:

- 2 whole eggs
- 100 g caster sugar
- 100 ml sweetened liquid cream
- 160 g flour
- 40 g almond flour (or flour)
- 50 g peeled almonds
- 1 sachet Baking powder

Directions:

1. Whip whole eggs with sugar by operating the high-speed electric whisks for at least 6 minutes. They should be clear and frothy. Add liquid cream and continue whipping at high speed. In this way you will see the cream "swell" the dough because in the meantime it is whipped.
2. Then Add almond flour and the sprinkle flour, incorporating them at low speed always with the electric whisk. Finally, Add baking powder and mix it with the dough.
3. Chop whole almonds, you can also use ready-made grain or Cut with a knife. Pour dough into a 20-22 cm donut mold and level it well. Sprinkle almonds on the surface making sure they stick to the dough.
4. Run fryer at 160 ° or in cake mode and Cook 18 minutes. Always check the cooking with a wooden toothpick.

Nutrition: Calories: 275; Fat:0.7g; Protein:24.2g; Carbs::11g

Minced Beef Steak with Ham

Preparation Time: 10 minutes
Cooking Time: 8 minutes
Servings: 2
Ingredients:

- 400 g minced beef
- 5 cm from the white part of a leek, very finely chopped
- 50 g of cooked haminutes in fine strips
- 3 tbsp. breadcrumbs
- Freshly ground pepper
- Nutmeg

Directions:

1. Preheat fryer 200 ° C. Mix minced beef with the leek, breadcrumbs, a little salt and pepper and the nutmeg. Knead well so that a uniform mass is created.
2. Divide the minced beef into four Servings: and shape into smooth minced steaks with wet hands.
3. Putminced steaks in the basket and slide the basket into the air fryer. Set timer to 8 minutes and fry the minced steaks until they are brown. Inside they can still be pink.
4. Serve beef steaks with boiled potatoes and cauliflower or broccoli.

Nutrition: Calories503 Protein13g Fat 22gCarbohydrates 62g

Jam Tart and Butter-Free Apples

Preparation Time: 15 minutes
Cooking Time: 20 minutes
Servings: 2
Ingredients:

- For the Oil Shortbread:
- 300 g flour 00
- 100 g caster sugar
- 2 eggs
- 70 ml Seed oil (corn or sunflower)
- 1 teaspoon baking powder
- For the stuffing
- 120 g cherry jam
- 2 red apples

Directions:

1. Prepare short crust pastry without butter following this recipe. You can also use it immediately; it does not require rest. Then, spread pastry on the lightly floured work surface and prepare a sheet of about half a centimeter. Leave some for the strips. Turn it upside down on the tart mold of 20-22 cm depending on the size of the basket of your air fryer.
2. use a perforated mold with removable bottom: in this way the air can circulate more easily and Cook tart faster. Spread jam and level it well. Peel apples, Remove core and Cut m into slices. Spread apples in rays on the jam. With remaining short crust pastry cut out strips with a smooth or toothed wheel.
3. Place strips on the tart and cook. Place mold directly on the basket and operate it at 160 ° or with the cake function. Cook 15 minutes and then another 5 minutes at 180 ° until golden brown, even on the bottom.
4. Bake preheated oven at 180 ° in static mode for about 40 minutes until golden brown, in the central shelf. Let it cool well before removing it from the mold. You can keep it for a maximum week wrapped in aluminum foil.

Nutrition: Calories: 567; Fat:22g; Protein:38g; Carbs::15g

Pork Satay with Peanut Sauce

Preparation Time: 35 minutes
Cooking Time: 10 m
Servings: 2
Ingredients:

- 2 cloves of garlic, crushed
- 2 cm fresh ginger root, grated, or 1 tsp ginger powder
- 2 tsp chili paste or hot pepper sauce
- 2 - 3 tbsp. sweet soy sauce
- 2 tablespoons vegetable oil
- 400 g lean pork chop, in 3 cm cubes
- 1 shallot, finely chopped
- 1 tsp ground coriander
- 200 ml coconut milk
- 100 g unsalted peanuts, ground

Directions:

1. Mix half of the garlic in a bowl with the ginger, 1 teaspoon of hot pepper sauce, 1 tablespoon of soy sauce and 1 tablespoon of oil. Mix meat with the mixture and marinate for 15 minutes.
2. Preheat fryer 200 ° C.
3. Place marinated meat in the basket and slide the basket into the Air fryer. Set timer to 12 minutes and roast the meat until it is brown and cooked. Turn once when roasting.
4. In the meantime, Prepare peanut sauce: Put 1 tablespoon of oil in a saucepan and briefly fry the shallot with the remaining garlic. Add coriander and continue to roast a little.
5. Mix coconut milk and the peanuts with 1 teaspoon of hot pepper sauce, 1 tablespoon of soy sauce and the shallot mixture and cook on a low flame for 5 minutes stirring. If the sauce becomes too thick, add a little water. Season it with soy sauce and hot pepper sauce.

Nutrition: Calories534 Protein12g Fat 27g Carbohydrates58g

Pineapple with Honey and Coconut

Preparation Time: 10 minutes
Cooking Time: 10-30 minutes
Servings: 2
Ingredients:

- ½ small, fresh pineapples
- 1 tbsp. honey
- ½ tbsp. lemon juice
- 1 tablespoon of ground coconut
- ¼ l ice cream or mango sorbet
- Baking paper

Directions:

1. Preheat fryer 200 ° C. Line the bottom of the basket with baking paper. Leave 1 cm on the edge.
2. Cut pineapple lengthwise into eight pieces and Remove peel with the "eyes". Also Remove woody middle trunk.
3. Mix honey with the lemon juice in a bowl. Brush pineapple pieces with the honey and add to the basket. Sprinkle coconut over it.
4. Push basket into the Air fryer and Set timer to 12 minutes. The pineapple with the coconut should be hot and golden brown.

Nutrition: Calories435 Protein 9g Fat 16g Carbohydrates61g

Beef, Pork and Lamb

— RECIPES —

Air Fried Grilled Steak

Preparation Time: 5 minutes
Cooking Time: 45 minutes
Servings: 2
Ingredients:
- 2 top sirloin steaks
- 3 tablespoons butter, melted
- 3 tablespoons olive oil
- Salt and pepper to taste

Directions:
1. Preheat Fryer 5 minutes. Season sirloin steaks with olive oil, salt and pepper.
2. Place beef in the air fryer basket.
3. Cook 45 minutes at 350°F.
4. Once cooked, serve with butter.

Nutrition: Calories 1536 Fat 123.7 g Carbs 0 g Protein 103.4 g

Air Fryer Beef Casserole

Preparation Time: 5 minutes
Cooking Time: 30 minutes
Servings: 2
Ingredients:
- 1 green bell pepper, seeded and chopped
- 1 onion, chopped
- 1-pound ground beef
- 3 cloves of garlic, minced
- 3 tablespoons olive oil
- 6 cups eggs, beaten
- Salt and pepper to taste

Directions:
1. Preheat the Air Fryer Oven for 5 minutes
2. In a baking dish that will fit in the air fryer, mix ground beef, onion, garlic, olive oil, and bell pepper. Season it with salt and pepper to taste.
3. Pour in the beaten eggs and give a good stir.
4. Place dish with the beef and egg mixture in the air fryer.
5. Pour into the Oven rack/basket. Place Rack on the middle-shelf of the Air Fryer Oven. Set temperature to 325°F, and set time to 30 minutes. Bake it for 30 minutes

Nutrition: Calories 1520 Cal Fat 125.11 g Carbs 0 g Protein 87.9 g

Apple pork tenderloin

Preparation Time: 10 minutes
Cooking Time: 14 to 19 minutes
Servings: 2
Ingredients:

- 1 (1-pound) pork tenderloin, cut into 4 pieces
- 1 tablespoon apple butter
- 2 teaspoons olive oil
- 2 granny smith apples or jonagold apples, sliced
- 3 celery stalks, sliced
- 1 onion, sliced
- ½ teaspoon dried marjoram
- ⅓ cup apple juice

Directions:

1. Rub each piece of pork with the apple butter and olive oil.
2. In a medium metal bowl, mix pork, apples, celery, onion, marjoram, and apple juice.
3. Place bowl into the air fryer and roast for 14 to 19 minutes, or until the pork reaches at least 145°f on a meat thermometer and the apples and vegetables are tender. Stir once during cooking. Serve immediately.

Nutrition: calories: 213; fat: 5g protein: 24g; Carbs: 20g;

Beef and broccoli

Preparation Time: 10 minutes
Cooking Time: 14 to 18 minutes
Servings: 2
Ingredients:

- 2 tablespoons cornstarch
- ½ cup low-sodium beef broth
- 1 teaspoon low-sodium soy sauce
- 12 ounces sirloin strip steak, cut into 1-inch cubes
- 2½ cups broccoli florets
- 1 onion, chopped
- 1 cup sliced cremini mushrooms
- 1 tablespoon grated fresh ginger
- Brown rice, cooked (optional)

Directions:

1. stir cornstarch, beef broth, and soy sauce. Add beef and toss to coat. Let stand for 5 minutes at room temperature.
2. With a slotted spoon, Transfer beef from the broth mixture into a medium metal bowl. ReServe broth.
3. Add broccoli, onion, mushrooms, and ginger to the beef. Place bowl into the air fryer and Cook 12 to 15 minutes, or until the beef reaches at least 145°f on a meat thermometer and the vegetables are tender.
4. Add reserved broth and cooked for 2 to 3 minutes more, or until the sauce boils.

Nutrition: calories: 240; fat: 6g protein: 19g; Carbs: 11g;

Beef Brisket Recipe from Texas

Preparation Time: 15 minutes
Cooking Time: 1 hour and 30 minutes
Servings: 2
Ingredients:

- 1 ½ cup beef stock
- 1 bay leaf
- 1 tablespoon garlic powder
- 1 tablespoon onion powder
- 2 pounds beef brisket, trimmed
- 2 tablespoons chili powder
- 2 teaspoons dry mustard
- 4 tablespoons olive oil
- Salt and pepper to taste

Directions:

1. Preheat the Air Fryer Oven for 5 minutes Place all ingredients in a deep baking dish that will fit in the air fryer.
2. Bake it for 1 hour and 30 minutes at 400°F.
3. Stir the beef every after 30 minutes to soak in the sauce.

Nutrition: Calories 306 Cal Fat 24.1 g Carbs 0 g Protein 18.3 g

Beef short ribs

Preparation Time: 10 minutes
Cooking Time: 35 minutes
Servings: 2
Ingredients

- 1 2/3 lbs. Short ribs
- Salt and black pepper, to taste
- 1 teaspoon grated garlic
- 1/2 teaspoon salt
- 1 teaspoon cumin seeds
- ¼ cup panko crumbs
- 1 teaspoon ground cumin
- 1 teaspoon avocado oil
- ½ teaspoon orange zest
- 1 egg, beaten

Directions:

1. Place beef ribs in a baking tray and Pour whisked egg on top. Whisk rest of the crusting ingredients in a bowl and spread over the beef. Press "power button" of air fry oven and turn the dial to select the "air fry" mode.
2. Press time button and again turn the dial to Set cooking time to 35 minutes.
3. Now Push temp button and rotate dial to Set temperature at 350 degrees f.
4. Once preheated, Place beef baking tray in the oven and close its lid.

Nutrition: Calories 267 fat 15.4 g carbs 58.5 g Protein 22.9 g

Copycat Taco Bell Crunch Wraps

Preparation Time: 10 minutes
Cooking Time: 2 minutes
Servings: 2
Ingredients:

- 6 wheat tostadas
- 2 C. sour cream
- 2 C. Mexican blend cheese
- 2 C. shredded lettuce
- 12 ounces low-sodium nacho cheese
- 3 Roma tomatoes
- 6 12-inch wheat tortillas
- 1 1/3 C. water
- 2 packets low-sodium taco seasoning
- 2 pounds of lean ground beef

Directions:

1. preheated fryer 400 degrees. Make beef according to taco seasoning packets.
2. Place 2/3 C. prepared beef, 4 tbsp. cheese, 1 tostada, 1/3 C. sour cream, 1/3 C. lettuce, 1/6th of tomatoes and 1/3 C. cheese on each tortilla.
3. Fold up tortillas edges and repeat with remaining ingredients. Lay folded sides of tortillas down into the air fryer and spray with olive oil.
4. Set temperature to 400°F, and set time to 2 minutes Cook 2 minutes till browned.

Nutrition: Calories 311 Fat 9 g Carbs 0 g Protein 22 g

Double cheeseburger

Preparation Time: 5 minutes
Cooking Time: 18 minutes
Servings: 2
Ingredients:

- 2 beef patties, pastured
- 1/8 teaspoon onion powder
- 2 slices of mozzarella cheese, low fat
- 1/8 teaspoon ground black pepper
- 1/8 teaspoon salt

Directions:

1. Switch air fryer, insert fryer basket, grease it with olive oil, then shut with its lid, Set fryer at 370 degrees f and preheat for 5 minutes.
2. Meanwhile, Season patties well with onion powder, black pepper, and salt.
3. Open fryer, add beef patties in it, close with its lid and Cook 12 minutes until nicely golden and cooked, flipping the patties halfway through the frying.
4. Then top the patties with a cheese slice and continue cooking for 1 minute or until cheese melts.

Nutrition: Calories: 670 cal Carbs: 0 g Fat: 50 g Protein: 39 g Carbs:0 g

Espresso-grilled pork tenderloin

Preparation Time: 15 minutes

Cooking Time: 9 to 11 minutes

Servings: 2

Ingredients:

- 1 tablespoon packed brown sugar
- 2 teaspoons espresso powder
- 1 teaspoon ground paprika
- ½ teaspoon dried marjoram
- 1 tablespoon honey
- 1 tablespoon freshly squeezed lemon juice
- 2 teaspoons olive oil
- 1 (1-pound) pork tenderloin

Directions:

1. mix brown sugar, espresso powder, paprika, and marjoram.
2. Stir honey, lemon juice, and olive oil until well mixed.
3. Spread honey mixture over the pork and let stand for 10 minutes at room temperature.
4. Roast tenderloin in the air fryer basket for 9 to 11 minutes, or until the pork registers at least 145°f on a meat thermometer. Slice the meat to serve.

Nutrition: calories: 177; fat: 5g protein: 23g; Carbs: 10g;

Greek vegetable skillet

Preparation Time: 10 minutes

Cooking Time: 9 to 19 minutes

Servings: 2

Ingredients:

- ½ pound 96 percent lean ground beef
- 2 medium tomatoes, chopped
- 1 onion, chopped
- 2 garlic cloves, minced
- 2 cups fresh baby spinach
- 2 tablespoons freshly squeezed lemon juice
- ⅓ cup low-sodium beef broth
- 2 tablespoons crumbled low-sodium feta cheese

Directions:

1. In a 6-by-2-inch metal pan, crumble the beef. **Cooking Time:** in the air fryer for 3 to 7 minutes, stirring once during cooking, until browned. Drain off any fat or liquid.
2. Add tomatoes, onion, and garlic to the pan. Air-fry for 4 to 8 minutes more, or until the onion is tender.
3. Add spinach, lemon juice, and beef broth. Air-fry for 2 to 4 minutes more, or until the spinach is wilted.
4. Sprinkle with feta cheese and serve immediately.

Nutrition: calories: 97; fat: 1g protein: 15g; Carbs: 5g;

Herbed lamb chops

Preparation Time: 1 hour and 10 minutes
Cooking Time: 13 minutes
Servings: 2
Ingredients:

- 1-pound lamb chops, pastured
- For the marinate:
- 2 tablespoons lemon juice
- 1 teaspoon dried rosemary
- 1 teaspoon salt
- 1 teaspoon dried thyme
- 1 teaspoon coriander
- 1 teaspoon dried oregano
- 2 tablespoons olive oil

Directions:

1. Prepare marinade and for this, place all its ingredients in a bowl and whisk until combined.
2. Pour marinade in a large plastic bag, add lamb chops in it, seal the bag, then turn it upside down to coat lamb chops with the marinade and let it marinate in the refrigerator for a minimum of 1 hour.
3. Then switch on fryer, insert fryer basket, grease it with olive oil, then shut with its lid, Set fryer at 390 degrees f and preheat for 5 minutes.
4. Meanwhile, Open fryer, add marinated lamb chops in it, close with its lid and Cook 8 minutes until nicely golden and cooked, turning the lamb chops halfway through the frying. When air fryer beeps, open its lid, transfer lamb chops onto a serving plate.

Nutrition: Calories: 177.4 cal Carbs: 1.7 g Fat: 8 g Protein: 23.4 g

Juicy Cheeseburgers

Preparation Time: 5 minutes
Cooking Time: 15 minutes
Servings: 2
Ingredients:

- 1 pound 93% lean ground beef
- 1 teaspoon Worcestershire sauce
- 1 tablespoon burger seasoning
- Salt
- Pepper
- Cooking oil
- 4 slices cheese
- Buns

Directions:

1. Mix ground beef, Worcestershire, burger seasoning, and salt and pepper to taste until well blended. Spray air fryer basket with cooking oil. You will need only a quick sprit. The burgers will produce oil as they cook. Shape the mixture into 4 patties. Place burgers in the air fryer. The burgers should fit without the need to stack, but stacking is okay if necessary.
2. Pour into the Oven rack/basket. Place Rack on the middle-shelf of the Air Fryer Oven. Set temperature to 375°F, and set time to 8 minutes Cook 8 minutes Open fryer and Flip burgers. Cook additional3 to 4 minutes Check the inside of the burgers to determine if they have finished cooking. You can stick a knife or fork in the center to examine the color.
3. Top each burger with a slice of cheese. Cook additionalminute, or until the cheese has melted
4. Serve on buns with any additional toppings of your choice.

Nutrition: Calories 566 Cal Fat 39 g Carbs 0 g Protein 29 g

Light herbed meatballs

Preparation Time: 10 minutes
Cooking Time: 12 to 17 minutes
Servings: 2
Ingredients:
- 1 medium onion, minced
- 2 garlic cloves, minced
- 1 teaspoon olive oil
- 1 slice low-sodium whole-wheat bread, crumbled
- 3 tablespoons 1 percent milk
- 1 teaspoon dried marjoram
- 1 teaspoon dried basil
- 1-pound 96 percent lean ground beef

Directions:
1. In a 6-by-2-inch pan, Combine onion, garlic, and olive oil. Air-fry for 2 to 4 minutes, or until the vegetables are crisp-tender.
2. Transfer vegetables to a medium bowl, and Add breadcrumbs, milk, marjoram, and basil. Mix well.
3. Add ground beef. With your hands, work the mixture gently but thoroughly until combined. Form meat mixture into about 24 (1-inch) meatballs.
4. Bake meatballs, in batches, in the air fryer basket for 12 to 17 minutes, or until they reach 160°f on a meat thermometer. Serve immediately.

Nutrition: calories: 190; fat: 6g protein: 25g; Carbs: 8g;

Mint lamb with roasted hazelnuts

Preparation Time: 10 minutes
Cooking Time: 25 minutes
Servings: 2
Ingredients
- ¼ cup hazelnuts, toasted
- 2/3 lb. Shoulder of lamb cut into strips
- 1 tablespoon hazelnut oil
- 2 tablespoon fresh mint leaves chopped
- ½ cup frozen peas
- ¼ cup of water
- ½ cup white wine
- Salt and black pepper to taste

Directions:
1. Toss lamb with hazelnuts, spices, and all ingredients in a baking pan. Press "power button" of air fry oven and turn the dial to select the "bake" mode.
2. Press time button and again turn the dial to Set cooking time to 25 minutes.
3. Now Push temp button and rotate dial to Set temperature at 370 degrees f.
4. Once preheated, Place baking pan in the oven and close its lid. Slice and serve warm.

Nutrition: Calories 322 fat 11.8 g carbs 14.6 g Protein 28 g

Pork Almond Bites

Preparation Time: 10 minutes
Cooking Time: 14 minutes
Servings: 2
Ingredients:
- 1-pound pork tenderloin
- 2 eggs
- 1 tsp butter
- ¼ cup almond flour
- 1 tsp kosher salt
- 1 tsp paprika
- 1 tsp ground coriander
- ½ tsp lemon zest

Directions:
1. Chop pork tenderloin into the large cubes Sprinkle pork cubes with the kosher salt, paprika, ground coriander, and lemon zest. Mix meat gently. Crack egg into a bowl and whisk it.
2. Coat meat cubes with the egg mixture and then the almond flour. Preheat fryer 365 F.
3. Put butter in the air fryer basket tray and then Place pork bites inside. Cook pork bites for 14 minutes.
4. Turn pork bites over after 7 minutes of cooking. When pork bites are cooked – serve them hot.

Nutrition: Calories 142, Fat 5.4g Carbs 0.6g
Protein 21.9g

Pork chops

Preparation Time: 5 minutes
Cooking Time: 15 minutes
Servings: 2
Ingredients:
- 4 slices of almond bread
- 5 pork chops, bone-in, pastured
- 3.5 ounces coconut flour
- 1 teaspoon salt
- 3 tablespoons parsley
- ½ teaspoon ground black pepper
- 1 tablespoon pork seasoning
- 2 tablespoons olive oil
- 1/3 cup apple juice, unsweetened
- 1 egg, pastured

Directions:
1. Switch on fryer, insert fryer basket, grease it with olive oil, then shut with its lid, Set fryer at 350 degrees f and preheat for 5 minutes. Meanwhile, place bread slices in a food processor and pulse until mixture resembles crumbs.
2. Tip breadcrumbs in a shallow dish, add parsley, ½ teaspoon salt, ¼ teaspoon ground black pepper and stir until mixed Place flour in another shallow dish, add remaining salt and black pepper, along with pork seasoning and stir until mixed.
3. Crack egg
4. Pour in apple juice and whisk until combined. Working on one pork chop at a time, first coat it into the flour mixture, then dip into egg and then evenly coat with breadcrumbs mixture.
5. Open fryer, add coated pork chops in it in a single layer, close with its lid and Cook 10 minutes until nicely golden and cooked, flipping the pork chops halfway through the frying. When air fryer beeps, open its lid, transfer pork chops onto a serving plate and serve.

Nutrition: Calories: 441 cal Carbs: 28.6 g Fat: 22.3 g
Protein: 30.6 g

Pork and fruit kebabs

Preparation Time: 15 minutes
Cooking Time: 9 to 12 minutes
Servings: 2
Ingredients:
- ⅓ cup apricot jam
- 2 tablespoons freshly squeezed lemon juice
- 2 teaspoons olive oil
- ½ teaspoon dried tarragon
- 1 (1-pound) pork tenderloin, cut into 1-inch cubes
- 4 plums, pitted and quartered
- 4 small apricots, pitted and halved

Directions:
1. mix jam, lemon juice, olive oil, and tarragon.
2. Add pork and stir to coat. Let stand for 10 minutes at room temperature.
3. Alternating the items, thread the pork, plums, and apricots onto 4 metal skewers that fit into the air fryer. Brush with any remaining jam mixture. Discard any remaining marinade.
4. Grill kebabs in the air fryer for 9 to 12 minutes, or until the pork reaches 145°f on a meat thermometer and the fruit is tender. Serve immediately.

Nutrition: calories: 256; fat; 5g protein: 24g; Carbs: 30g;

Pork and mixed greens salad

Preparation Time: 10 minutes
Cooking Time: 15 minutes
Servings: 2
Ingredients:
- 2 pounds pork tenderloin, cut into 1-inch slices
- 1 teaspoon olive oil
- 1 teaspoon dried marjoram
- ⅛ teaspoon freshly ground black pepper
- 6 cups mixed salad greens
- 1 red bell pepper, sliced
- 1 (8-ounce) package button mushrooms, sliced
- ⅓ cup low-sodium low-fat vinaigrette dressing

Directions:
1. mix pork slices and olive oil. Toss to coat.
2. Sprinkle with the marjoram and pepper and Rub se into the pork.
3. Grill pork in the air fryer, in batches, for about 4 to 6 minutes, or until the pork reaches at least 145°f on a meat thermometer.
4. Meanwhile, in a serving bowl, mix salad greens, red bell pepper, and mushrooms. Toss gently.
5. When pork is cooked, Add slices to the salad. drizzle with the vinaigrette and toss gently. Serve immediately.

Nutrition: calories: 172; fat: 5 g protein: 27g; Carbs: 28g;

Poultry

— RECIPES —

Chicken coconut meatballs

Preparation Time: 10 minutes
Cooking Time: 10 minutes
Servings: 2
Ingredients:
- 1 lb. Ground chicken
- 1 ½ tsp sriracha
- 1/2 tbsp soy sauce
- 1/2 tbsp hoisin sauce
- ¼ cup shredded coconut
- 1 tsp sesame oil
- ½ cup fresh cilantro, chopped
- 2 green onions, chopped
- Pepper
- Salt

Directions:
1. Sprayir fryer basket with cooking spray.
2. Add all ingredients into the large bowl and mix until well combined.
3. Make small balls from meat mixture and place into the air fryer basket.
4. Cook at 350 f for 10 minutes. Turn halfway through.

Nutrition: Calories 255 Fat 11 g Carbohydrates 3 g Protein 32 g

Chicken In Bacon Wrap

Preparation Time: 5 minutes
Cooking Time: 15 minutes
Servings: 2
Ingredients:
- 2 chicken breasts
- 8 ounces (227 g) onion and chive cream cheese
- 6 slices turkey bacon
- 1 tablespoon fresh parsley, chopped
- Juice from ½ lemon
- From the Cupboard:
- 1 tablespoon butter
- Salt, to taste
- Special Equipment:
- 2 or 4 toothpicks, soaked for at least 30 minutes

Directions:
1. Preheat fryer 390°F (199°C). Spritz fryer basket with cooking spray. On a clean work surface, Brush chicken breasts with cream cheese and butter on both sides. Sprinkle with salt.
2. Wrap each chicken breast with 3 slices of bacon and secure with 1 or 2 toothpicks.
3. Arrange bacon-wrapped chicken in the preheated air fryer and Cook 14 minutes or until the bacon is well browned and a meat thermometer inserted in the chicken reads at least 165°F (74°C). Flipm halfway through the cooking time.
4. Removem from fryer basket and serve with parsley and lemon juice on top.

Nutrition: Calories: 437 Fat: 28.6g Carbs: 5.2g Protein: 39.8g

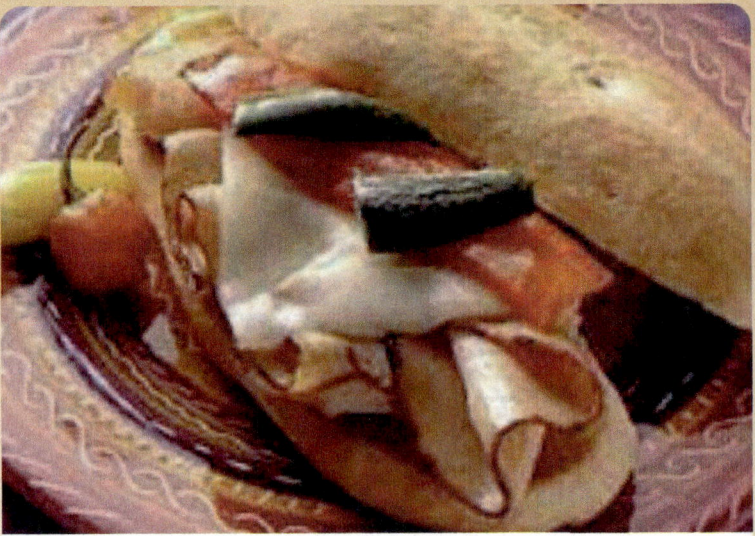

Cheese herb chicken wings

Preparation Time: 10 minutes
Cooking Time: 15 minutes
Servings: 2
Ingredients:
- 2 lbs. Chicken wings
- 1 tsp herb de provence
- ½ cup parmesan cheese, grated
- 1 tsp paprika
- Salt

Directions:
1. Preheat fryer 350 f.
2. mix together cheese, herb de provence, paprika, and salt.
3. Spray fryer basket with cooking spray.
4. Toss chicken wings with cheese mixture and place into the air fryer basket and Cook 15 minutes. Turn halfway through.

Nutrition: Calories 505 Fat 20 g Carbohydrates 0.4 g Protein 70 g

Turkey And Pepper Sandwich

Preparation Time: 5 minutes
Cooking Time: 5 minutes
Servings: 2
Ingredients:
- 2 slices whole grain bread
- 2 teaspoons Dijon mustard
- 2 ounces (57 g) cooked turkey breast, thinly sliced
- 2 slices low-fat Swiss cheese
- 3 strips roasted red bell pepper

From the Cupboard:
- Salt and ground black pepper, to taste

Directions:
1. Preheat fryer 330°F (166°C). Spritz fryer basket with cooking spray. Assemble sandwich: On a dish, place a slice of bread, then top the bread with 1 teaspoon of Dijon mustard, use a knife to smear the mustard evenly.
2. Layer the turkey slices, Swiss cheese slices, and red pepper strips on the bread according to your favorite order. Top them with remaining teaspoon of Dijon mustard and remaining bread slice.
3. Place sandwich in the preheated air fryer and spritz with cooking spray. Sprinkle with salt and black pepper. Cook 5 minutes until the cheese melts and the bread is lightly browned. Flip sandwich halfway through the cooking time.

Nutrition: Calories: 328 Fat: 5.0g Carbs: 38.0g Protein: 29.0g

Cheesy Spinach Stuffed Chicken Breasts

Preparation Time: 20 minutes
Cooking Time: 25 minutes
Servings: 2
Ingredients:
- 1 (10-ounce / 284-g) package frozen spinach, thawed and drained well
- 1 cup feta cheese, crumbled
- 4 boneless chicken breasts
- From the Cupboard:
- Salt and ground black pepper, to taste
- Special Equipment:
- 4 or 8 toothpicks, soaked for at least 30 minutes

Directions:
1. Preheat fryer 380°F (193°C). Spritz fryer basket with cooking spray.
2. Make the filling: Chop spinach and Put in a large bowl, then Add feta cheese and ½ teaspoon of ground black pepper. Stir to mix well.
3. On a clean work surface, using a knife, cut a 1-inch incision into the thicker side of each chicken breast horizontally. Make a 3-inch long pocket from the incision and keep the sides and bottom intact.
4. Stuff chicken pockets with the filling and secure with 1 or 2 toothpicks.
5. Arrange stuffed chicken breasts in the preheated air fryer. Sprinkle with salt and black pepper and spritz with cooking spray. You may need to work in batches to avoid overcrowding.
6. Cook 12 minutes or until the internal temperature of the chicken reads at least 165°F (74°C). Flip chicken halfway through the cooking time.
7. Remove chicken from the air fryer basket. Discard toothpicks and cool before slicing to serve.

Nutrition: Calories: 648 Fat: 38.7g Carbs: 4.5g Protein: 68.2g

Chicken and Zucchini

Preparation Time: 30 minutes
Cooking Time: 20 minutes
Servings: 2
Ingredients:
- 1/4 cup olive oil
- 1 tablespoon lemon juice
- 2 tablespoons red wine vinegar
- 1 teaspoon oregano
- 1 tablespoon garlic, chopped
- 2 chicken breast fillet, sliced into cubes
- 1 zucchini, sliced
- 1 red onion, sliced
- 1 cup cherry tomatoes, sliced
- Salt and pepper to taste

Directions:
1. mix olive oil, lemon juice, vinegar, oregano and garlic. Pour half of mixture into another bowl.
2. Toss chicken in half of the mixture. Cover and marinate for 15 minutes. Toss veggies in the remaining mixture.
3. Season both chicken and veggies with salt and pepper. Add chicken to the air fryer basket.
4. Spread veggies on top. Select air fry function. Seal and cook at 380 degrees f for 15 to 20 minutes.

Nutrition: Calories: 282 kcal Protein: 21.87 g Fat: 19.04 g Carbs: 5.31 g

Chicken kabab

Preparation Time: 10 minutes
Cooking Time: 6 minutes
Servings: 2

Ingredients:
- 1 lb. Ground chicken
- 1 tbsp fresh lemon juice
- ¼ cup almond flour
- 2 green onion, chopped
- 1 egg, lightly beaten
- 1/3 cup fresh parsley, chopped
- 3 garlic cloves
- 4 oz onion, chopped
- ¼ tsp turmeric powder
- ½ tsp pepper

Directions:
1. Add all ingredients into the food processor and process until well combined.
2. Transfer chicken mixture to the bowl and place in the refrigerator for 1 hour.
3. Divide mixture into the 6 equal portions and roll around the soaked wooden skewers.
4. Sprayir fryer basket with cooking spray. Place skewers into the air fryer basket and cooks at 400 f for 6 minutes.

Nutrition: Calories 290 Fat 7 g Carbohydrates 6 g Protein 48 g

Chicken, Mushroom, And Pepper Kabobs

Preparation Time: 1 hour 5 minutes
Cooking Time: 15-20 minutes
Servings: 2

Ingredients:
- ⅓ cup raw honey
- 2 tablespoons sesame seeds
- 2 boneless chicken breasts, cut into cubes
- 6 white mushrooms, cut in halves
- 3 green or red bell peppers, diced

From the Cupboard:
- ⅓ cup soy sauce
- Salt and ground black pepper, to taste
- Special Equipment:
- 4 wooden skewers, soaked for at least 30 minutes

Directions:
1. Combine honey, soy sauce, sesame seeds, salt, and black pepper in a large bowl. Stir to mix well. Dunk the chicken cubes in this bowl, then wrap the bowl in plastic and refrigerate to marinate for at least an hour.
2. Preheat fryer 390°F (199°C). Spritz fryer basket with cooking spray. Remove chicken cubes from the marinade, then run the skewers through the chicken cubes, mushrooms, and bell peppers alternatively.
3. Baste chicken, mushrooms, and bell peppers with the marinade, then Arrange m in the preheated air fryer.
4. Spritz them with cooking Spraynd Cook 15 to 20 minutes or until the mushrooms and bell peppers are tender and the chicken cubes are well browned. Flipm halfway through the cooking time. Transfer skewers to a large plate and serve hot.

Nutrition: Calories: 380 Fat: 16.0g Carbs: 26.1g Protein: 34.0g

Chicken Thighs With Honey-Dijon Sauce

Preparation Time: 5 minutes
Cooking Time: 35 minutes
Servings: 2
Ingredients:
- 8 bone-in and skinless chicken thighs
- Chicken seasoning or rub, to taste
- ½ cup honey
- ¼ cup Dijon mustard
- 2 garlic cloves, minced
- From the Cupboard:
- Salt and ground black pepper, to taste

Directions:
1. Preheat fryer 400°F (205°C). Spritz fryer basket with cooking spray. On a clean work surface, Rub chicken thighs with chicken seasoning, salt, and black pepper.
2. Cook chicken thighs in the preheated air fryer for 15 minutes or until the internal temperature of the chicken thighs reaches at least 165°F (74°C). Flip thighs halfway through the cooking time. You may need to work in batches to avoid overcrowding.
3. Meanwhile, Combine honey, Dijon mustard, and garlic in a saucepan, and cook over medium-high heat for 3 to 4 minutes until the sauce reduced by one third. Keep stirring during the cooking.
4. Remove chicken thighs from the air fryer basket and Put on a dish. Baste thighs with the cooked sauce and serve warm.

Nutrition: Calories: 382 Fat: 18.0g Carbs: 36.0g Protein: 21.0g

Chicken tenders

Preparation Time: 10 minutes
Cooking Time: 12 minutes
Servings: 2
Ingredients:
- 1 lb. Chicken tenders
- 1 egg, lightly beaten
- 3/4 cup pecans, crushed
- ¼ cup ground mustard
- ½ tsp paprika
- ¼ tsp garlic powder
- ¼ tsp onion powder
- 1/4 tsp pepper
- 1 tsp salt

Directions:
1. Sprayir fryer basket with cooking spray. Add chicken into the large bowl. Season with paprika, pepper, garlic powder, onion powder, and salt. Add mustard mix well.
2. In a separate bowl, add egg and whisk well. In a shallow bowl, add crushed pecans.
3. Dip chicken into the egg then coats with pecans and place into the air fryer basket.
4. Cook at 350 f for 12 minutes.

Nutrition: Calories 481 Fat 31 g Carbohydrates 7 g Protein 40 g

Chicken Wings with Sweet Chili Sauce

Preparation Time: 6 minutes
Cooking Time: 14 minutes
Servings: 2

Ingredients:
- 1-pound (454 g) chicken wings
- 1 teaspoon garlic powder
- 1 tablespoon tamarind powder
- ¼ cup sweet chili sauce
- From the Cupboard:
- Salt and ground black pepper, to taste

Directions:
1. Preheat fryer 390°F (199°C). Spritz fryer with cooking spray.
2. On a clean work surface, Rub chicken wings with garlic powder, tamarind powder, salt, and black pepper.
3. Place wings in the basket and Cook 6 minutes, then spread chili sauce on top and Cook additional 8 minutes or until the internal temperature of the wings reaches at least 165°F (74°C).
4. Remove wings from the air fryer. Allow to cool for a few minutes and serve.

Nutrition: Calories: 165 Fat: 4.1g Carbs: 4.5g Protein: 25.5g

Crunchy Golden Nuggets

Preparation Time: 5 minutes
Cooking Time: 10 minutes
Servings: 2

Ingredients:
- 2 chicken breasts, cut into nuggets
- 4 tablespoons sour cream
- ½ cup bread crumbs
- ½ tablespoon garlic powder

From the Cupboard:
- ½ teaspoon cayenne pepper
- Salt and ground black pepper, to taste

Directions:
1. Preheat fryer 360°F (182°C). Spritz fryer basket with cooking spray.
2. Put sour cream in a large bowl. Combine bread crumbs, cayenne pepper, garlic powder, salt, and black pepper on a large plate.
3. Dredge chicken nuggets in the bowl of sour cream, shake the excess off, then roll the nuggets through the bread crumbs mixture to coat well.
4. Place nuggets in the air fryer basket and Cook 10 minutes or until the chicken nuggets are golden brown and crispy. Flip nuggets halfway through the cooking time. Remove nuggets from basket and serve warm.

Nutrition: Calories: 324 Fat: 15.5g Carbs: 11.7g Protein: 32.7g

Delicious chicken tenderloins

Preparation Time: 10 minutes
Cooking Time: 15 minutes
Servings: 2
Ingredients:
- 1 egg, lightly beaten
- ¼ cup heavy whipping cream
- 8 oz chicken breast tenderloins
- 1 cup almond flour
- ¼ tsp garlic powder
- ¼ tsp onion powder
- 1 tsp pepper
- 1 tsp salt

Directions:
1. Whisk egg, with garlic powder, onion powder, cream, pepper, and salt in a bowl.
2. In a dish, Add almond flour. Dip chicken in egg mixture then coats with almond flour mixture.
3. Sprayir fryer basket with cooking spray.
4. Place chicken into the air fryer basket and cook at 450 f for 15 minutes.

Nutrition: Calories 255 Fat 6 g Carbohydrates 2 g Protein 45 g

Easy Paprika Chicken

Preparation Time: 7 minutes
Cooking Time: 18 minutes
Servings: 2
Ingredients:
- 4 chicken breasts
- 1 tablespoon paprika
- ¼ teaspoon garlic powder
- 2 tablespoons fresh thyme, chopped
- From the cupboard:
- Salt and ground black pepper, to taste
- 2 tablespoons butter, melted

Directions:
1. Preheat fryer 360°F (182°C). Spritz fryer basket with cooking spray.
2. On a clean work surface, Rub chicken breasts with paprika, garlic powder, salt, and black pepper, then brush with butter.
3. Cook chicken in the preheated air fryer for 18 minutes or until the internal temperature reaches at least 165°F (74°C). Flip chicken with tongs halfway through the cooking time.
4. Serve cooked chicken on a plate immediately with thyme on top.

Nutrition: Calories: 368 Fat: 14.1g Carbs: 2.3g Protein: 57.9g

Garlic herb chicken breasts

Preparation Time: 10 minutes
Cooking Time: 15 minutes
Servings: 2
Ingredients:
- 2 lbs. Chicken breasts, skinless and boneless
- 4 garlic cloves, minced
- ¼ cup yogurt
- ¼ cup mayonnaise
- 2 tsp garlic herb seasoning
- 1/2 tsp onion powder
- ¼ tsp salt

Directions:
1. Preheat fryer 380 f. mix mayonnaise, seasoning, onion powder, garlic, and yogurt.
2. Brush chicken with mayo mixture and season with salt.
3. Sprayir fryer basket with cooking spray.
4. Place chicken into the air fryer basket and Cook 15 minutes.

Nutrition: Calories 410 Fat 16 g Carbohydrates 5 g Protein 55 g

Italian Chicken And Cheese Frittata

Preparation Time: 25 minutes ago
Cooking Time: 20 minutes
Servings: 2
Ingredients:
- 1 (1-pound) fillet chicken breast
- Sea salt and ground black pepper, to taste
- 1 tablespoon olive oil
- 4 eggs
- 1/2 teaspoon cayenne pepper
- 1/2 cup Mascarpone cream
- 1/4 cup Asiago cheese, freshly grated

Directions:
1. Flatten chicken breast with a meat mallet. Season with salt and pepper. Heat olive oil. Cook chicken for 10 to 12 minutes; slice into small strips, and reserve.
2. Combine eggs, and cayenne pepper; season with salt to taste. Add cheese and stir to combine.
3. Add reserved chicken. Then, Pour mixture into a lightly greased pan; Putpan into the cooking basket.
4. Cook in the preheated Air Fryer at 355 degrees F for 10 minutes, flipping over halfway through.

Nutrition: Calories: 330 cal Carbs: 3 g Fat: 21 g Protein: 32 g

Lemon and Honey Glazed Game Hen

Preparation Time: 10 minutes
Cooking Time: 20 minutes
Servings: 2
Ingredients:
- 1 (2-pound / 907-g) Cornish game hen, split in half
- ¼ teaspoon dried thyme
- Juice and zest of 1 lemon
- ¼ cup honey
- 1½ teaspoons chopped fresh thyme leaves
- From the Cupboard:
- 1 tablespoon olive oil
- Salt and ground black pepper, to taste
- ½ teaspoon soy sauce

Directions:
1. Preheat fryer 390°F (199°C). Spritz fryer basket with cooking spray. On a clean work surface, Brush game hen halves with olive oil, then sprinkle with dried thyme, salt, and black pepper to season.
2. Cook hen in the preheated air fryer for 15 minutes or until the hen is lightly browned. Flip hen halfway through. Meanwhile, mix lemon juice and zest, honey, thyme leaves, soy sauce, and black pepper in a bowl.
3. Baste game hen with the honey glaze, then Cook additional 4 minutes or until the hen is well glazed and a meat thermometer inserted in the hen reads at least 165°F (74°C).
4. Remove game hen from the air fryer basket. Allow to cool for a few minutes and slice to serve.

Nutrition: Calories: 724 Fat: 22.0g Carbs: 37.5g Protein: 91.3g

Mediterranean chicken

Preparation Time: 10 minutes
Cooking Time: 35 minutes
Servings: 2
Ingredients:
- 4 lbs. Whole chicken, cut into pieces
- 2 tsp ground sumac
- 2 garlic cloves, minced
- 2 lemons, sliced
- 2 tbsp olive oil
- 1 tsp lemon zest
- 2 tsp kosher salt

Directions:
1. Rub chicken with oil, sumac, lemon zest, and salt. Place in the refrigerator for 2-3 hours.
2. Add lemon sliced into the air fryer basket top with marinated chicken.
3. Cook at 350 for 35 minutes.
4. Serve and enjoy.

Nutrition: Calories 616 Fat 27 g Carbohydrates 0.4 g Protein 87 g

Parmigiana Chicken

Preparation Time: 3 minutes
Cooking Time: 12 minutes
Servings: 2
Ingredients:
- 2 eggs
- ½ cup Parmesan cheese, grated
- 1 cup seasoned bread crumbs
- 1-pound (454 g) chicken breast halves
- 2 sprigs rosemary, chopped
- From the cupboard:
- Salt and ground black pepper, to taste

Directions:
1. Preheat fryer 380°F (193°C). Spritz fryer basket with cooking spray. Beat egg in a first bowl and sprinkle with salt and black pepper. Combine Parmesan and bread crumbs in the second bowl.
2. Dredge chicken in the first bowl to coat well, then in the second the bowl. Shake the excess off.
3. Cook chicken in the preheated air fryer for 12 minutes or until the internal temperature reaches at least 165°F (74°C). Flip chicken halfway through the cooking time.
4. Transfer chicken to a plate and serve with rosemary on top.

Nutrition: Calories: 430 Fat: 25.0g Carbs: 21.5g Protein: 48.0g

Roasted Whole Chicken

Preparation Time: 10 minutes
Cooking Time: 40 minutes
Servings: 2
Ingredients:
- 1 (3-pound / 1.4-kg) chicken, rinsed and patted dry
- 1 garlic bulb
- 1 sprig fresh tarragon
- 1 lemon, cut into wedges
- From the Cupboard:
- 2 tablespoons butter, melted
- Salt and ground black pepper, to taste

Directions:
1. Preheat fryer 380°F (193°C). Spritz fryer basket with cooking spray.
2. On a clean work surface, Brush chicken with butter and rub with salt and black pepper. Stuff chicken with garlic, tarragon, and lemon wedges.
3. Arrange chicken in the air fryer basket and roast for 40 minutes or until an instant-read thermometer inserted in the thickest part of the chicken registers at least 165°F (74°C).
4. Remove chicken from the basket and Put on a large platter. Carve the chicken and slice to serve.

Nutrition: Calories: 440 Fat: 15.0g Carbs: 2.6g Protein: 69.7g

Seafood

— RECIPES —

Air fried cod with basil vinaigrette

Preparation Time: 5 minutes
Cooking Time: 15 minutes
Servings: 2
Ingredients:
- ¼ cup olive oil
- 4 cod fillets
- A bunch of basil, torn
- Juice from 1 lemon, freshly squeezed
- Salt and pepper to taste

Directions:
1. Preheat fryer for 5 minutes. Season cod fillets with salt and pepper to taste.
2. Place in fryer and Cook 15 minutes at 3500f.
3. Meanwhile, mix rest of the ingredients in a bowl and toss to combine.
4. Serve air fried cod with the basil vinaigrette.

Nutrition: Calories 235; Carbs: 1.9g; protein: 14.3g; fat: 18.9g

Air Fryer Fish Tacos

Preparation Time: 5 minutes
Cooking Time: 15 minutes
Servings: 2
Ingredients:
- 1-pound cod
- 1 tbsp. cumin
- ½ tbsp. chili powder
- 1 ½ cup of almond flour
- 1 ½ cup of coconut flour
- 10 ounces' Mexican beer
- 2 eggs

Directions:
1. Whisk beer and eggs together.
2. Whisk flours, pepper, salt, cumin, and chili powder together. Slice cod into large pieces and coat in egg mixture then flour mixture.
3. Spray bottom of your air fryer basket with olive oil and add coated codpieces.
4. Cook 15 minutes at 375 degrees. Serve on lettuce leaves topped with homemade salsa!

Nutrition: Calories: 178 Fat: 10g Protein: 19g Carbs: 2.1g

Air fryer salmon patties

Preparation Time: 8 minutes
Cooking Time: 7 minutes
Servings: 2
Ingredients:
- 1 tbsp. Olive oil
- 1 tbsp. Ghee
- ¼ tsp. Salt
- 1/8 tsp. Pepper
- 1 egg
- 1 c. Almond flour
- 1 can wild alaskan pink salmon

Directions:
1. Drain can of salmon into a bowl and keep liquid. Discard skin and bones.
2. Add salt, pepper, and egg to salmon, mixing well with hands to incorporate. Make patties.
3. Dredge in flour and remaining egg. If it seems dry, spoon reserved salmon liquid from the can onto patties.
4. Pour patties into the oven rack/basket. Place rack on the middle-shelf of the air fryer oven. Set temperature to 378°f and set time to 7 minutes. Cook 7 minutes till golden, making sure to flip once during cooking process.

Nutrition: calories: 437; carbs:55; fat: 12g; protein:24g;

Almond flour coated crispy shrimps

Preparation Time: 5 Minutes
Cooking Time: 10 minutes
Servings: 2
Ingredients:
- ½ cup almond flour
- 1 tablespoon yellow mustard
- 1-pound raw shrimps, peeled and deveined
- 3 tablespoons olive oil
- Salt and pepper to taste

Directions:
1. place all ingredients in a ziploc bag and give a good shake.
2. place in the fryer and Cook 10 minutes at 4000f.

Nutrition: Calories 206; Carbs: 1.3g; protein: 23.5g; fat: 11.9g

Seafood | 51

Apple slaw topped alaskan cod filet

Preparation Time: 5 Minutes

Servings: 2

Cooking Time: 15 minutes

Ingredients:

- ¼ cup mayonnaise
- ½ red onion, diced
- 1 ½ pounds frozen alaskan cod
- 1 box whole wheat panko breadcrumbs
- 1 granny smith apple, julienned
- 1 tablespoon vegetable oil
- 1 teaspoon paprika
- 2 cups napa cabbage, shredded
- Salt and pepper to taste

Directions:

1. Preheat fryer 3900f. Place grill pan accessory in the air fryer.
2. Brush fish with oil and dredge in the breadcrumbs.
3. Place fish on the grill pan and Cook 15 minutes. Make sure to Flip fish halfway through the cooking time.
4. Meanwhile, Prepare slaw by mixing the remaining ingredients in a bowl. Serve fish with the slaw.

Nutrition: Calories 316; carbs: 13.5g; protein: 37.8g; fat: 12.2g

Bacon Wrapped Scallops

Preparation Time: 10 minutes

Cooking Time: 6 minutes

Servings: 2

Ingredients:

- 1 tsp. paprika
- 1 tsp. lemon pepper
- 5 slices of center-cut bacon
- 20 raw sea scallops

Directions:

1. Rinse and drain scallops, placing on paper towels to soak up excess moisture. Cut slices of bacon into 4 pieces.
2. Wrap each scallop with a piece of bacon, using toothpicks to secure. Sprinkle wrapped scallops with paprika and lemon pepper.
3. Sprayir fryer basket with olive oil and add scallops.
4. Cook 5-6 minutes at 400 degrees, making sure to flip halfway through.

Nutrition: Calories: 389 Fat: 17g Protein: 21g Carbs: 11g

Baked cod fillet recipe from thailand

Preparation Time: 5 Minutes
Cooking Time: 20 minutes
Servings: 2
Ingredients:
- ¼ cup coconut milk, freshly squeezed
- 1 tablespoon lime juice, freshly squeezed
- 1-pound cod fillet, cut into bite-sized pieces
- Salt and pepper to taste

Directions:
1. Preheat fryer for 5 minutes.
2. Place all ingredients in a baking dish that will fit in the air fryer.
3. Place in fryer.
4. Cook 20 minutes at 3250f.

Nutrition: Calories 844; Carbs: 2.3g; protein: 21.6g; fat: 83.1g

Baked scallops with garlic aioli

Preparation Time: 5 minutes
Cooking Time: 10 minutes
Servings: 2
Ingredients:
- 1 cup breadcrumbs
- 1/4 cup chopped parsley
- 16 sea scallops, rinsed and drained
- 2 shallots, chopped
- 3 pinches ground nutmeg
- 4 tablespoons olive oil
- 5 cloves garlic, minced
- 5 tablespoons butter, melted
- Salt and pepper to taste

Directions:
1. Lightly grease baking pan of air fryer with cooking spray.
2. Mix in shallots, garlic, melted butter, and scallops. Season with pepper, salt, and nutmeg.
3. whisk well olive oil and breadcrumbs. Sprinkle over scallops.
4. For 10 minutes, cook on 390of until tops are lightly browned. Serve and enjoy with a sprinkle of parsley.

Nutrition: Calories 452; carbs: 29.8g; protein: 15.2g; fat: 30.2g

Basil 'n lime-chili clams

Preparation Time: 5 Minutes
Cooking Time: 15 minutes
Servings: 2

Ingredients:
- ½ cup basil leaves
- ½ cup tomatoes, chopped
- 1 tablespoon fresh lime juice
- 25 littleneck clams
- 4 cloves of garlic, minced
- 6 tablespoons unsalted butter
- Salt and pepper to taste

Directions:
1. Preheat fryer 3900f.
2. Place grill pan accessory in the air fryer.
3. On a large foil, place all ingredients. Fold over the foil and close by crimping the edges.
4. Place on grill pan and Cook 15 minutes. Serve with bread.

Nutrition: Calories 163; carbs: 4.1g; protein: 1.7g; fat: 15.5g

Bass filet in coconut sauce

Preparation Time: 5 Minutes
Cooking Time: 15 minutes
Servings: 2

Ingredients:
- ¼ cup coconut milk
- ½ pound bass fillet
- 1 tablespoon olive oil
- 2 tablespoons jalapeno, chopped
- 2 tablespoons lime juice, freshly squeezed
- 3 tablespoons parsley, chopped
- Salt and pepper to taste

Directions:
1. Preheat fryer for 5 minutes. Season bass with salt and pepper to taste
2. Brush surface with olive oil. Place in fryer and Cook 15 minutes at 3500f.
3. Meanwhile, place in a saucepan, the coconut milk, lime juice, jalapeno and parsley.
4. Heat over medium flame. Serve fish with the coconut sauce.

Nutrition: Calories 139; Carbs: 2.7g; protein: 8.7g; fat: 10.3

Beer battered cod filet

Preparation Time: 5 Minutes
Cooking Time: 15 minutes
Servings: 2
Ingredients:
- ½ cup all-purpose flour
- ¾ teaspoon baking powder
- 1 ¼ cup lager beer
- 2 cod fillets
- 2 eggs, beaten
- Salt and pepper to taste

Directions:
1. Preheat fryer 390ºf.
2. Pat fish fillets dry then set aside.
3. Combine rest of the ingredients to create a batter.
4. Dip fillets on the batter and place on the double layer rack. Cook 15 minutes.

Nutrition: Calories 229; carbs: 33.2g; protein: 31.1g; fat: 10.2g

Buttered baked cod with wine

Preparation Time: 5 Minutes
Cooking Time: 12 minutes
Servings: 2
Ingredients:
- 1 tablespoon butter
- 1 tablespoon butter
- 2 tablespoons dry white wine
- 1/2 pound thick-cut cod loin
- 1-1/2 teaspoons chopped fresh parsley
- 1-1/2 teaspoons chopped green onion
- 1/2 lemon, cut into wedges
- 1/4 sleeve buttery round crackers (such as ritz®), crushed
- 1/4 lemon, juiced

Directions:
1. melt butter in microwave. Whisk in crackers. Lightly grease baking pan of air fryer with remaining butter. And melt for 2 minutes at 390ºf.
2. whisk lemon juice, white wine, parsley, and green onion.
3. Coat cod filets in melted butter. Pour dressing. Top with butter-cracker mixture.
4. Cook 10 minutes at 390ºf. Serve and enjoy with a slice of lemon.

Nutrition: Calories 266; carbs: 9.3g; protein: 20.9g; fat: 16.1g

Buttered garlic-oregano on clams

Preparation Time: 5 Minutes
Cooking Time: 5 minutes
Servings: 2

Ingredients:
- ¼ cup parmesan cheese, grated
- ¼ cup parsley, chopped
- 1 cup breadcrumbs
- 1 teaspoon dried oregano
- 2 dozen clams, shucked
- 3 cloves of garlic, minced
- 4 tablespoons butter, melted

Directions:
1. mix breadcrumbs, parmesan cheese, parsley, oregano, and garlic. Stir melted butter.
2. Preheat fryer 3900f.
3. Place baking dish accessory in the air fryer and Place clams.
4. Sprinkle crumb mixture over the clams. Cook 5 minutes.

Nutrition: Calories 160; carbs: 6.3g; protein: 2.9g; fat: 13.6g

Butterflied prawns with garlic-sriracha

Preparation Time: 5 Minutes
Cooking Time: 15 minutes
Servings: 2

Ingredients:
- 1 tablespoon lime juice
- 1 tablespoon sriracha
- 1-pound large prawns, shells removed and cut lengthwise or butterflied
- 1teaspoon fish sauce
- 2 tablespoons melted butter
- 2 tablespoons minced garlic
- Salt and pepper to taste

Directions:
1. Preheat fryer 3900f.
2. Place grill pan accessory in the air fryer.
3. Season prawns with the rest of the ingredients.
4. Place on grill pan and Cook 15 minutes. Make sure to Flip prawns halfway through the cooking time.

Nutrition: Calories 443; carbs:9.7 g; protein: 62.8g; fat: 16.9g

Cajun seasoned salmon filet

Preparation Time: 5 Minutes

Cooking Time: 15 minutes

Servings: 2

Ingredients:
- 1 salmon fillet
- 1 teaspoon juice from lemon, freshly squeezed
- 3 tablespoons extra virgin olive oil
- A dash of cajun seasoning mix
- Salt and pepper to taste

Directions:
1. Preheat fryer for 5 minutes.
2. Place all ingredients in a bowl and toss to coat.
3. Place fish fillet in the air fryer basket.
4. Bake for 15 minutes at 3250f. Once cooked drizzle with olive oil

Nutrition: Calories Nutrition: 523; Carbs: 4.6g; protein: 47.9g; fat: 34.8g

Cajun spiced lemon-shrimp kebabs

Preparation Time: 5 Minutes

Cooking Time: 10 minutes

Servings: 2

Ingredients:
- 1 tsp cayenne
- 1 tsp garlic powder
- 1 tsp kosher salt
- 1 tsp onion powder
- 1 tsp oregano
- 1 tsp paprika
- 12 pcs xl shrimp
- 2 lemons, sliced thinly crosswise
- 2 tbsp olive oil

Directions:
1. mix all ingredients except for sliced lemons. Marinate for 10 minutes.
2. Thread 3 shrimps per steel skewer. Place in air fryer.
3. Cook 5 minutes at 390of.
4. Serve and enjoy with freshly squeezed lemon.

Nutrition: Calories Nutrition: 232; carbs: 7.9g; protein: 15.9g; fat: 15.1g

Cajun spiced veggie-shrimp bake

Preparation Time: 5 Minutes
Cooking Time: 20 minutes
Servings: 2

Ingredients:
- 1 bag of frozen mixed vegetables
- 1 tbsp gluten free cajun seasoning
- Olive oil spray
- Season with salt and pepper
- Small shrimp peeled & deveined (regular size bag about 50-80 small shrimp)

Directions:
1. Lightly grease baking pan of air fryer with cooking spray. Add all ingredients and toss well to coat. Season with pepper and salt, generously.
2. For 10 minutes, cook on 330of. Halfway through cooking time, stir.
3. Cook 10 minutes at 330of.
4. Serve and enjoy.

Nutrition: Calories nutrition: 78; carbs: 13.2g; protein: 2.8g; fat: 1.5g

Coconut shrimp

Preparation Time: 5 minutes
Cooking Time: 10 minutes
Servings: 2

Ingredients:
- 1 c. Almond flour
- 1 c. Panko breadcrumbs
- 1 tbsp. Coconut flour
- 1 c. Unsweetened, dried coconut
- 1 egg white
- 12 raw large shrimp

Directions:
1. Put shrimp on paper towels to drain.
2. Mix coconut and panko breadcrumbs together. Then mix in coconut flour and almond flour in a different bowl. Set to the side.
3. Dip shrimp into flour mixture, then into egg white, and then into coconut mixture.
4. Place into air fryer basket. Repeat with remaining shrimp. Set temperature to 350°f and set time to 10 minutes. Turn halfway through cooking process.

Nutrition: calories:213; fat: 8g; protein:15g; carbs: 13g

Crispy Air Fried Sushi Roll

Preparation Time: 15 minutes
Cooking Time: 10 minutes
Servings: 2
Ingredients:

- Kale Salad:
- 1 tbsp. sesame seeds
- ¾ tsp. soy sauce
- ¼ tsp. ginger
- 1/8 tsp. garlic powder
- ¾ tsp. toasted sesame oil
- ½ tsp. rice vinegar
- 1 ½ cup chopped kale
- Sushi Rolls:
- ½ of a sliced avocado
- 3 sheets of sushi nor
- 1 batch cauliflower rice
- Sriracha Mayo:
- Sriracha sauce
- ¼ cup vegan mayo
- Coating:
- ½ cup panko breadcrumbs

Directions:

1. Combine all of kale salad ingredients together, tossing well. Set to the side.
2. Lay out a sheet of nor and spread a handful of rice on. Then place 2-3 tbsp. of kale salad over rice, followed by avocado. Roll up sushi. To make mayo, whisk mayo ingredients together until smooth.
3. Add breadcrumbs to a bowl. Coat sushi rolls in crumbs till coated and add to air fryer.
4. Cook rolls 10 minutes at 390 degrees, shaking gently at 5 minutes. Slice each roll into 6-8 pieces and enjoy!

Nutrition: Calories: 267 Fat: 13g Protein: 6g Carbs: 3g

Fried Calamari

Preparation Time: 15 minutes
Cooking Time: 15 minutes
Servings: 2
Ingredients:

- ½ tsp. salt
- ½ tsp. Old Bay seasoning
- 1/3 cup plain cornmeal
- ½ cup semolina flour
- ½ cup almond flour
- 5-6 cup olive oil
- 1 ½ pounds baby squid

Directions:

1. Rinse squid in cold water and slice tentacles, keeping just ¼-inch of the hood in one piece.
2. Combine 1-2 pinches of pepper, salt, Old Bay seasoning, cornmeal, and both flours together. Dredge squid pieces into flour mixture and place into air fryer. Spray liberally with olive oil.
3. Cook 15 minutes at 345 degrees till coating turns a golden brown.

Nutrition: Calories: 211 Fat: 6g Protein: 21g Carbs: 11g

Vegetables and Salad

— RECIPES —

Air Fried Leeks

Preparation Time: 10 minutes
Cooking Time: 7 minutes
Servings: 2
Ingredients:
- 2 leeks, washed, ends cut, and halved
- Salt and black pepper, to taste
- ½ tablespoon butter, melted
- ½ tablespoon lemon juice

Directions:
1. Rub leeks with melted butter and season with salt and pepper.
2. Lay it inside fryer and cook at 350F for 7 minutes.
3. Arrange on platter. Drizzle with lemon juice and serve.

Nutrition: Calories: 100 Fat: 4g Carb: 6g Protein: 2g

Asparagus and Parmesan

Preparation Time: 10 minutes
Cooking Time: 6 minutes
Servings: 2
Ingredients:
- 1 teaspoon sesame oil
- 11 oz asparagus
- 1 teaspoon chicken stock
- ½ teaspoon ground white pepper
- 3 oz Parmesan

Directions:
1. Wash asparagus and chop it roughly. Sprinkle chopped asparagus with the chicken stock and ground white pepper. Then Sprinkle vegetables with the sesame oil and shake them.
2. Place asparagus in the air fryer basket. Cook vegetables for 4 minutes at 400 F. Meanwhile, shred Parmesan cheese.
3. When time is over – shake the asparagus gently and sprinkle with the shredded cheese. Cook asparagus for 2 minutes more at 400 F.
4. After this, Transfer cooked asparagus in the serving plates.

Nutrition: Calories 189, Fat 11.6, Carbs 7.9 Protein 17.2

Vegetables and salad | 61

Asparagus with Garlic

Preparation Time: 5 minutes
Cooking Time: 10 minutes
Servings: 2
Ingredients:

- 1-pound asparagus, rinsed, ends snapped off where they naturally break (see Tip)
- 2 teaspoons olive oil
- 3 garlic cloves, minced
- 2 tablespoons balsamic vinegar
- ½ teaspoon dried thyme

Directions:

1. mix asparagus with olive oil. ¬Transfer to air fryer basket.
2. Sprinkle with garlic. Roast 4 to 5 minutes for crisp-tender or for 8 to 11 minutes for asparagus that is crisp on the outside and tender on the inside.
3. Drizzle with balsamic vinegar and sprinkle with the thyme leaves. Serve immediately.

Nutrition: Calories: 41; Fat: 1g Protein: 3g; Carbs: 6g;

Brussel Sprout Salad

Preparation Time: 20 minutes
Cooking Time: 15 minutes
Servings: 2
Ingredients:

- For Salad:
- 1 pound fresh medium Brussels sprouts, trimmed and halved vertically
- 3 teaspoons olive oil
- Salt and ground black pepper, as required
- 2 apples, cored and chopped
- 1 red onion, sliced
- 4 cups lettuce, torn
- For Dressing:
- 2 tablespoons extra-virgin olive oil
- 2 tablespoons fresh lemon juice
- 1 tablespoon apple cider vinegar
- 1 tablespoon honey
- 1 teaspoon Dijon mustard
- Salt and ground black pepper, as required

Directions:

1. Set temperature of fryer to 360 degrees F.
2. For Brussels sprout: Add Brussels sprout, oil, salt, and black pepper and toss to coat well. Spread Brussels sprouts onto a large baking sheet. Arrange baking sheet into air fryer basket and air fryer for about 15 minutes, flipping once halfway through.
3. Remove from air fryer and Transfer Brussel sprouts onto a plate. Set aside to cool slightly. mix together the Brussel sprouts, apples, onion, and lettuce.
4. For dressing: add all ingredients and beat until well combined. Add dressing and gently, stir to combine.

Nutrition: Calories: 235 Carbs: 34.5g Protein: 4.9g Fat: 11.3g

Caramelized Carrots

Preparation Time: 10 minutes
Cooking Time: 15 minutes
Servings: 2
Ingredients:
- ½ cup butter, melted
- ½ cup brown sugar
- 1 small bag baby carrots

Directions:
1. Set temperature of fryer to 400 degrees F. Grease fryer basket. mix together the butter and brown sugar.
2. Add carrots and coat well. Arrange carrots into the prepared air fryer basket in a single layer.
3. Air fry for about 15 minutes.
4. Remove from air fryer and Transfer carrots onto serving plates.

Nutrition: Calories: 416 Carbs: 36.2g Protein: 1.3g Fat: 30.9g

Cauliflower Salad

Preparation Time: 20 minutes
Cooking Time: 10 minutes
Servings: 2
Ingredients:

For Salad
- ¼ cup golden raisins
- 1 cup boiling water
- ¼ cup olive oil
- 1 head cauliflower, cut into small florets
- 1 tablespoon curry powder
- Salt, to taste
- ¼ cup pecans, toasted and chopped
- 2 tablespoons fresh mint leaves, chopped

For Dressing:
- 1 cup mayonnaise
- 2 tablespoons sugar
- 1 tablespoon fresh lemon juice

Directions:
1. For salad: Add cauliflower, curry powder, salt, and oil and toss to coat well. Set temperature of air fryer to 390 degrees F. Grease an air fryer basket. Arrange cauliflower florets into the prepared air fryer basket in a single layer. Air fry for about 8-10 minutes.
2. Meanwhile, Add raisins, and boiling water and set aside until using. Remove from air fryer and Transfer cauliflower florets onto a plate. Set aside to cool. Drain raisins well.
3. For dressing: add all ingredients and mix until well combined. mix together the cauliflower, raisins and pecans. Add dressing and gently, stir to combine.
4. Refrigerate to chill before serving. Garnish with mint and serve

Nutrition: Calories: 162 Carbs: 25.3g Protein: 11.3g Fat: 3.1g

Chard with Cheddar

Preparation Time: 10 minutes
Cooking Time: 11 minutes
Servings: 2
Ingredients:
- 3 oz Cheddar cheese, grated
- 10 oz Swiss chard
- 3 tablespoon cream
- 1 tablespoon sesame oil
- salt and pepper to taste

Directions:
1. Wash Swiss chard carefully and chop it roughly. After this, sprinkle chopped Swiss chard with the salt and ground white pepper. Stir it carefully. Sprinkle Swiss chard with the sesame oil and stir it carefully with the help of 2 spatulas.
2. Preheat fryer 260 F. Put chopped Swiss chard in the air fryer basket and Cook 6 minutes. Shake after 3 minutes of cooking. Then Pour cream into the air fryer basket and mix it up.
3. Cook meal for 3 minutes more. Then Increase temperature to 400 F.
4. Sprinkle meal with the grated cheese and Cook 2 minutes more. After this, Transfer meal in serving plates. Enjoy!

Nutrition: Calories 272, Fat 22.3, Carbs 6.7, Protein 13.3

Cheesy Brussel Sprouts

Preparation Time: 15 minutes
Cooking Time: 10 minutes
Servings: 2
Ingredients:
- 1 pound Brussels sprouts, trimmed and halved
- 1 tablespoon balsamic vinegar
- 1 tablespoon extra-virgin olive oil
- Salt and ground black pepper, as required
- ¼ cup whole wheat breadcrumbs
- ¼ cup Parmesan cheese, shredded

Directions:
1. Set temperature of fryer to 400 degrees F. Grease fryer basket. mix well Brussel sprouts, vinegar, oil, salt, and black pepper.
2. Arrange Brussel sprouts into the prepared air fryer basket in a single layer. Air fry for about 5 minutes.
3. Remove from air fryer and Flip Brussel sprouts. Sprinkle Brussel sprouts evenly with breadcrumbs, followed by the cheese.
4. Air fryer for about 5 more minutes. Remove from air fryer and Transfer Brussels sprouts onto serving plates.

Nutrition: Calories: 240 Carbs: 19.4g Protein: 16.3g Fat: 12.6

Cheesy Roasted Sweet Potatoes

Preparation Time: 5 minutes
Cooking Time: 20 minutes
Servings: 2
Ingredients:
- 2 large sweet potatoes, peeled and sliced
- 1 teaspoon olive oil
- 1 tablespoon white balsamic vinegar
- 1 teaspoon dried thyme
- ¼ cup grated Parmesan cheese

Directions:
1. Shower sweet potato slices with the olive oil and toss. Sprinkle with balsamic vinegar and thyme and toss again.
2. Sprinkle potatoes with the Parmesan cheese and toss to coat.
3. Roast the slices, in batches, in the air fryer basket for 18 to 23 minutes, tossing the sweet potato slices in the basket once during cooking, until tender.
4. Repeat with the remaining sweet potato slices. Serve immediately.

Nutrition: Calories: 100; Fat: 3g Protein: 4g; Carbs: 15g;

Chili Squash Wedges

Preparation Time: 10 minutes
Cooking Time: 18 minutes
Servings: 2
Ingredients:
- 11 oz Acorn squash
- ½ teaspoon salt
- tablespoon olive oil
- ½ teaspoon chili pepper
- ½ teaspoon paprika

Directions:
1. Cut Acorn squash into the serving wedges. Sprinkle wedges with the salt, olive oil, chili pepper, and paprika.
2. Massage wedges gently. Preheat fryer 400 F.
3. Put Acorn squash wedges in the air fryer basket and Cook 18 minutes.
4. Flip wedges into another side after 9 minutes of cooking.

Nutrition: Calories 125, Fat 7.2, Carbs 16.7, Protein 1.4

Corn on Cobs

Preparation Time: 10 minutes
Cooking Time: 10 minutes
Servings: 2
Ingredients:
- 2 fresh corn on cobs
- 2 teaspoon butter
- 1 teaspoon salt
- 1 teaspoon paprika
- ¼ teaspoon olive oil

Directions:
1. Preheat fryer 400 F. Rub corn on cobs with the salt and paprika.
2. Then Sprinkle corn on cobs with the olive oil. Place corn on cobs in the air fryer basket.
3. Cook corn on cobs for 10 minutes.
4. When the time is over – Transfer corn on cobs in the serving plates and rub with the butter gently.

Nutrition: Calories 122, Fat 5.5, Carbs 17.6, Protein 3.2

Cream Potato

Preparation Time: 15 minutes
Cooking Time: 20 minutes
Servings: 2
Ingredients:
- 3 medium potatoes, scrubbed
- ½ teaspoon kosher salt
- 1 tablespoon Italian seasoning
- 1/3 cup cream
- ½ teaspoon ground black pepper

Directions:
1. Slice potatoes. Preheat fryer 365 F. Make layer from the sliced potato in the air fryer basket.
2. Sprinkle potato layer with salt and pepper. After this, make the second layer of the potato and sprinkle it with Italian seasoning.
3. Make last layer of the sliced potato and Pour cream. Cook scallop potato for 20 minutes.
4. When the scalloped potato is cooked – let it chill till the room temperature. Enjoy!

Nutrition: Calories 269, Fat 4.7, Carbs 52.6, Protein 5.8

Crispy Broccoli

Preparation Time: 10 minutes
Cooking Time: 10 minutes
Servings: 2
Ingredients:
- 1 large head fresh broccoli
- 2 teaspoons olive oil
- tablespoon lemon juice

Directions:
1. Rinse broccoli and pat dry. Cut off the florets and Separate m. You can also use the broccoli stems too; Cut m into 1" chunks and Peelm.
2. Toss broccoli, olive oil, and lemon juice in a large bowl until coated.
3. Roast broccoli in the air fryer, in batches, for 10 to 14 minutes or until the broccoli is crisp-tender and slightly brown around the edges. Repeat with the remaining broccoli. Serve immediately.

Nutrition: Calories: 63; Fat: 2g Protein: 4g; Carbs: 10g;

Crispy Brussels Sprouts and Potatoes

Preparation Time: 10 minutes
Cooking Time: 8 minutes
Servings: 2
Ingredients:
- ¾ pound brussels sprouts, washed and trimmed
- ½ cup new potatoes, chopped
- 2 teaspoons bread crumbs
- Salt and black pepper, to taste
- 2 teaspoons butter

Directions:
1. add Brussels sprouts, potatoes, bread crumbs, salt, pepper, and butter. Mix well.
2. Place in fryer and cook at 400F for 8 minutes.
3. Serve.

Nutrition: Calories: 152 Fat: 3g Carb: 17g Protein: 4g

Dill Mashed Potato

Preparation Time: 10 minutes
Cooking Time: 15 minutes
Servings: 2
Ingredients:
- 2 potatoes
- 2 tablespoon fresh dill, chopped
- 1 teaspoon butter
- ½ teaspoon salt
- ¼ cup half and half

Directions:
1. Preheat fryer 390 F. Rinse potatoes thoroughly and Place in fryer. Cook potatoes for 15 minutes.
2. After this, Remove potatoes from the air fryer. Peel potatoes. Mash potatoes with the help of the fork well.
3. Then add chopped fresh dill and salt. Stir it gently and add butter and half and half.
4. Take the hand blender and blend the mixture well. When mashed potato is cooked – serve it immediately. Enjoy!

Nutrition: Calories 211, Fat 5.7, Carbs 36.5, Protein 5.1

Eggplant Salad

Preparation Time: 15 minutes
Cooking Time: 15 minutes
Servings: 2
Ingredients:
For Salad:
- 1 eggplant, cut into ½-inch-thick slices crosswise
- 2 tablespoons canola oil
- Salt and ground black pepper, as required
- 1 avocado, peeled, pitted and chopped
- 1 teaspoon fresh lemon juice

For Dressing:
- 1 tablespoon extra-virgin olive oil
- 1 tablespoon red wine vinegar
- 1 tablespoon honey
- 1 tablespoon fresh oregano leaves, chopped
- 1 teaspoon fresh lemon zest, grated
- 1 teaspoon Dijon mustard
- Salt and ground black pepper, as required

Directions:
1. Set temperature of air fryer to 400 degrees F. Grease an air fryer basket.
2. For salad: Add eggplant, oil, salt, and black pepper and toss to coat well. Arrange eggplants pieces into the prepared air fryer basket in a single layer. Air fry for about 15 minutes, shaking after every 5 minutes.
3. Remove from air fryer and Transfer eggplant pieces onto a plate. Set aside to cool slightly. mix together the avocado and lemon juice. In a serving bowl, mix together the eggplants pieces and avocado mixture.
4. For dressing: add all ingredients and beat until well combined. Add dressing and gently, stir to combine.

Nutrition: Calories: 489 Carbs: 32.7g Protein: 4.6g Fat: 41.4g

Green Beans and Cherry Tomatoes

Preparation Time: 10 minutes
Cooking Time: 15 minutes
Servings: 2
Ingredients:
- 8 ounces cherry tomatoes
- 8 ounces green beans
- 1 tablespoon olive oil
- Salt and black pepper, to taste

Directions:
1. mix cherry tomatoes with green beans, olive oil, salt, and pepper. Mix.
2. Cook in fryer at 400 degrees F for 15 minutes. Shake once.
3. Serve.

Nutrition: Calories: 162 Fat: 6g Carb: 8g Protein: 9g

Garlic-Roasted Bell Peppers

Preparation Time: 5 minutes
Cooking Time: 20 minutes
Servings: 2
Ingredients:
- 4 bell peppers, any colors, stemmed, seeded, membranes removed, and cut into fourths
- 1 teaspoon olive oil
- 4 garlic cloves, minced
- ½ teaspoon dried thyme

Directions:
1. Put peppers in the basket of the air fryer and drizzle with olive oil. Toss gently. Roast 15 minutes.
2. Sprinkle with garlic and thyme. Roast 3 to 5 minutes more, or until tender. Serve immediately.

Nutrition: Calories: 36; Fat: 1g Protein: 1g; Carbs: 5g;

Honey Glazed Carrots

Preparation Time: 15 minutes
Cooking Time: 12 minutes
Servings: 2
Ingredients:
- 3 cups carrots, peeled and cut into large chunks
- 1 tablespoon olive oil
- 1 tablespoon honey
- 1 tablespoon fresh thyme, finely chopped
- Salt and ground black pepper, as required

Directions:
1. Set temperature of fryer to 390 degrees F. Grease fryer basket. mix well carrot, oil, honey, thyme, salt, and black pepper.
2. Arrange carrot chunks into the prepared air fryer basket in a single layer.
3. Air fry for about 12 minutes.
4. Remove from air fryer and Transfer carrot chunks onto serving plates.

Nutrition: Calories: 82 Carbs: 12.9g Protein: 0.8g Fat: 3.6g

Mixed Veggie Salad

Preparation Time: 25 minutes
Cooking Time: 1 hour 35 minutes
Servings: 2
Ingredients:
- 2 tablespoons olive oil, divided
- 3 medium zucchinis, sliced into ½-inch thick rounds
- 3 small eggplants, sliced into ½-inch thick rounds
- 4 medium tomatoes, cut in eighths
- 1 cup cherry tomatoes, quartered
- 2 red bell peppers, seeded and chopped
- 4 fresh basil leaves, chopped
- ½ cup Italian dressing
- Salt, as required
- ½ cup Parmesan cheese, grated

Directions:
1. Set temperature of fryer to 355 degrees F. Grease fryer basket. mix zucchini and one tablespoon of oil.
2. Place zucchini slices into the prepared air fryer basket. Air fry for about 25 minutes. Remove from fryer and Place zucchini slices into a bowl. Set aside. mix eggplant and one tablespoon of oil.
3. Place eggplant slices into the greased air fryer basket. Air fry for about 30-40 minutes. Remove from air fryer and Place eggplant slices into a bowl with zucchini. Set aside. Now, Set temperature of air fryer to 320 degrees F.
4. Place tomatoes into the greased air fryer basket. Air fry for about 30 minutes. Remove from air fryer and Place tomatoes into a bowl with veggies. Add bell pepper, basil, salt, dressing, and salt and gently, stir to combine. Cover the bowl of salad and refrigerate for 2 hours before serving. Garnish with Parmesan cheese and serve.

Nutrition: Calories: 179 Carbs: 21.6g Protein: 6g Fat: 9.6g

Measurements Conversion

CONVERSION CHART

Liquid Measure

8 ounces =	1 cup
2 cups =	1 pint
16 ounces =	1 pint
4 cups =	1 quart
1 gill =	1/2 cup or 1/4 pint
2 pints =	1 quart
4 quarts =	1 gallon
31.5 gal. =	1 barrel
3 tsp =	1 tbsp
2 tbsp =	1/8 cup or 1 fluid ounce
4 tbsp =	1/4 cup
8 tbsp =	1/2 cup
1 pinch =	1/8 tsp or less
1 tsp =	60 drops

Conversion of US Liquid Measure to Metric System

1 fluid oz. =	29.573 milliliters
1 cup =	230 milliliters
1 quart =	.94635 liters
1 gallon =	3.7854 liters
.033814 fluid ounce =	1 milliliter
3.3814 fluid ounces =	1 deciliter
33.814 fluid oz. or 1.0567 qt.=	1 liter

Dry Measure

2 pints =	1 quart
4 quarts =	1 gallon
8 quarts =	2 gallons or 1 peck
4 pecks =	8 gallons or 1 bushel
16 ounces =	1 pound
2000 lbs. =	1 ton

Conversion of US Weight and Mass Measure to Metric System

.0353 ounces =	1 gram
1/4 ounce =	7 grams
1 ounce =	28.35 grams
4 ounces =	113.4 grams
8 ounces =	226.8 grams
1 pound =	454 grams
2.2046 pounds =	1 kilogram
.98421 long ton or 1.1023 short tons =	1 metric ton

Linear Measure

12 inches =	1 foot
3 feet =	1 yard
5.5 yards =	1 rod
40 rods =	1 furlong
8 furlongs (5280 feet) =	1 mile
6080 feet =	1 nautical mile

Conversion of US Linear Measure to Metric System

1 inch =	2.54 centimeters
1 foot =	.3048 meters
1 yard =	.9144 meters
1 mile =	1609.3 meters or 1.6093 kilometers
.03937 in. =	1 millimeter
.3937 in.=	1 centimeter
3.937 in.=	1 decimeter
39.37 in.=	1 meter
3280.8 ft. or .62137 miles =	1 kilometer

To convert a Fahrenheit temperature to Centigrade, do the following:
a. Subtract 32   b. Multiply by 5   c. Divide by 9

To convert Centigrade to Fahrenheit, do the following:
a. Multiply by 9   b. Divide by 5   c. Add 32

Recipes Index

Breakfast

Best Air-Fried English Breakfast	20
Breakfast Grilled Ham and Cheese	20
Breakfast Scramble Casserole	21
Cheesy Tater Tot Breakfast Bake	21
Classic Hash Browns	22
Creamy and cheesy pancake	22

Snacks and Appetizers

Apple and Greek Yogurt Cake Baked	24
Buckwheat and Forest Berries	24
Cake Gluten Free and Lactose Free	24
Chocolate and Hazelnut Cake	25
Donut Cream and Almonds	25
Minced Beef Steak with Ham	26
Jam Tart and Butter-Free Apples	26
Pork Satay with Peanut Sauce	27
Pineapple with Honey and Coconut	27
Air Fried Grilled Steak	29
Air Fryer Beef Casserole	29
Apple pork tenderloin	30
Beef and broccoli	30
Beef Brisket Recipe from Texas	31
Beef short ribs	31
Copycat Taco Bell Crunch Wraps	32
Double cheeseburger	32
Espresso-grilled pork tenderloin	33
Greek vegetable skillet	33
Herbed lamb chops	34
Juicy Cheeseburgers	34
Light herbed meatballs	35
Mint lamb with roasted hazelnuts	35
Pork Almond Bites	36
Pork chops	36
Pork and fruit kebabs	37
Pork and mixed greens salad	37

Poultry

Chicken coconut meatballs	39
Chicken In Bacon Wrap	39
Cheese herb chicken wings	40
Turkey And Pepper Sandwich	40
Cheesy Spinach Stuffed Chicken Breasts	41
Chicken and Zucchini	41
Chicken kabab	42
Chicken, Mushroom, And Pepper Kabobs	42
Chicken Thighs With Honey-Dijon Sauce	43
Chicken tenders	43
Chicken Wings with Sweet Chili Sauce	44
Crunchy Golden Nuggets	44
Delicious chicken tenderloins	45
Easy Paprika Chicken	45
Garlic herb chicken breasts	46
Italian Chicken And Cheese Frittata	46
Lemon and Honey Glazed Game Hen	47
Mediterranean chicken	47
Parmigiana Chicken	48
Roasted Whole Chicken	48

Seafood

Air fried cod with basil vinaigrette	50
Air Fryer Fish Tacos	50
Air fryer salmon patties	51
Almond flour coated crispy shrimps	51
Apple slaw topped alaskan cod filet	52
Bacon Wrapped Scallops	52
Baked cod fillet recipe from thailand	53
Baked scallops with garlic aioli	53
Basil 'n lime-chili clams	54
Bass filet in coconut sauce	54
Beer battered cod filet	55
Buttered baked cod with wine	55
Buttered garlic-oregano on clams	56
Butterflied prawns with garlic-sriracha	56
Cajun seasoned salmon filet	57
Cajun spiced lemon-shrimp kebabs	57
Cajun spiced veggie-shrimp bake	58
Coconut shrimp	58
Crispy Air Fried Sushi Roll	59
Fried Calamari	59

Vegetables and Salad

Air Fried Leeks	61
Asparagus and Parmesan	61
Asparagus with Garlic	62
Brussel Sprout Salad	62
Caramelized Carrots	63
Cauliflower Salad	63
Chard with Cheddar	64
Cheesy Brussel Sprouts	64
Cheesy Roasted Sweet Potatoes	65
Chili Squash Wedges	65
Corn on Cobs	66
Cream Potato	66
Crispy Broccoli	67
Crispy Brussels Sprouts and Potatoes	67
Dill Mashed Potato	68
Eggplant Salad	68
Green Beans and Cherry Tomatoes	69
Garlic-Roasted Bell Peppers	69
Honey Glazed Carrots	70
Mixed Veggie Salad	70

Conclusion

To conclude the discussion of the air fryer, it can be said to be one of the best inventions in both technology and power in recent years.

It can also be said that it is possible to cook a myriad of recipes that we are usually accustomed to making fried, or baked, without particular difficulty, achieving the exact same result.

Therefore, it becomes an essential purchase since it is not only an excellent ally in the kitchen, but also of our health itself.

It has been repeatedly stated in this text that it is possible to make excellent light, crispy, and tasty fried foods with just one tablespoon of oil (as much as 85% less fat).

Compared to frying, using an air fryer can reduce the amount of fat, calories and potentially harmful compounds in food only benefiting our health.

Printed in Great Britain
by Amazon

85693578R00045